Bring Science Alive!
Exploring Science Practices

TCi™

NEXT GENERATION
SCIENCE
STANDARDS*
For States, By States

Chief Executive Officer
Bert Bower

Chief Operating Officer
Amy Larson

Director of Product Development
Maria Favata

Strategic Product Manager
Nathan Wellborne

Senior Science Content Developer
Ariel Stein

Curriculum Consultants
Kim Merlino
Joan Westley

Program Editors
David Fraker
Mikaila Garfinkel
Edward Helderop
Rebecca Ou
Ginger Wu

Editorial Consultant
Glenda Stewart

Production Manager
Jodi Forrest

Operations & Software Manager
Marsha Ifurung

Designer
Sarah Osentowski

Art Direction
Julia Foug

TCi™

Teachers' Curriculum Institute
PO Box 1327
Rancho Cordova, CA 95741

Customer Service: 800-497-6138
www.teachtci.com

ISBN 978-1-58371-973-2
2 3 4 5 6 7 8 9 10 -WC- 20 19 18 17 16 15

Manufactured by Webcrafters, Inc., Madison, WI
United States of America, May 2015, Job # 121651

SUSTAINABLE FORESTRY INITIATIVE
Certified Sourcing
www.sfiprogram.org
SFI-00617

About the Next Generation Science Standards

What Teachers and Families Need to Know

The Next Generation Science Standards (NGSS) describe the science skills and knowledge all students need to know to succeed in college, careers, and citizenship. The standards were developed by a panel that collaborated with representatives from 26 lead states. They are based on *A Framework for K–12 Science Education*, which was written by a team of scientists, engineers, and science educators, and published by the National Research Council in 2012.

The NGSS were released in Spring 2013, and TCI's science instructional program, *Bring Science Alive!*, was developed to meet them.

Each performance expectation has three dimensions: disciplinary core ideas, scientific and engineering practices, and crosscutting concepts. Together, these describe what students should understand and be able to accomplish at each grade level.

What are performance expectations, and how does *Bring Science Alive!* prepare students to demonstrate mastery?

Performance expectations describe what all students should be able to do at the completion of a unit of study. They guide assessment and are supported by the details in the disciplinary core ideas, practices, and crosscutting concepts. Many performance expectations are followed by clarification statements and assessment boundaries. Clarification statements provide examples and details, and assessment boundaries limit what students should be tested on.

Performance expectation 4-LS1-1. has students construct an argument that internal and external structures function to support the survival, behavior, reproduction, and growth of plants and animals.

Bring Science Alive! prepares students to meet the performance expectations. Performance expectations are identified in the Student Text at the beginning of each unit and each lesson. They are also incorporated into the investigations in the online Presentations for students to practice.

How are the Next Generation Science Standards related to Common Core standards?

The NGSS are aligned to the Common Core State Standards for English Language Arts & Literacy in History/ Social Studies, Science, and Technical Subjects and Common Core State Standards for Mathematics.

Similarly, *Bring Science Alive!* is aligned to Common Core English and Mathematics. For example, all Reading Furthers in the Student Text align with the Reading Standards for Informational Text K–5. Interactive Tutorials address Common Core reading and writing standards. Lesson content and investigations are aligned with Common Core Mathematics, such as when students learn about measurement units and tools and graphing.

What are Disciplinary Core Ideas, and how does *Bring Science Alive!* meet them?

Disciplinary core ideas focus instruction on the foundational knowledge students need for success in each grade. Core ideas build from year to year, from Kindergarten to Grade 12, in learning progressions that revisit each topic several times, each time with greater depth and sophistication. Therefore, students are expected to understand the core ideas that were taught in previous grades.

For these reasons, teachers and parents may find fewer topics taught in each grade than they have seen previously. Additionally, many topics are taught in different grades than they were under previous standards. By limiting the content at each grade, students are able to learn with deeper understanding.

Bring Science Alive! guides students through these core ideas as they read their Student Text, complete Interactive Tutorials, carry out hands-on and online investigations, and write, draw, diagram, and calculate in their Interactive Student Notebooks.

One part of the disciplinary core idea PS2.A: Forces and Motion focuses on observing and measuring the patterns of an object's motion in different situations so that the object's motion can be predicted in future situations.

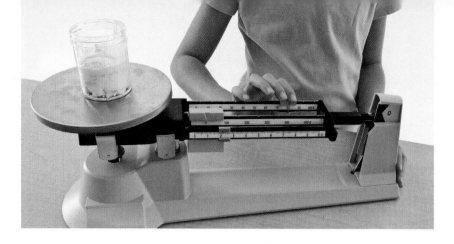

What are Science and Engineering Practices, and how does *Bring Science Alive!* meet them?

Science and engineering practices describe the abilities students should develop to engage in science and engineering. Students use these eight practices to master the principles described in the core ideas. The practices also help students understand how professional scientists and engineers answer questions and solve problems.

- **?** Asking questions and defining problems
- Developing and using models
- **Q** Planning and carrying out investigations
- Analyzing and interpreting data
- Using mathematics and computational thinking
- Constructing explanations and designing solutions
- Engaging in argument from evidence
- Obtaining, evaluating, and communicating information

The science and engineering practice Engaging in Argument from Evidence asks students to use data, evidence, and models to support an argument they make.

Every lesson in *Bring Science Alive!* develops several science and engineering practices in the online lesson Presentation. Practices are used explicitly and help teach the lesson's core ideas. Each of the eight practices is taught at every grade level with increasing sophistication from grade to grade.

What are Crosscutting Concepts, and how does *Bring Science Alive!* meet them?

The crosscutting concepts are used to organize students' understanding of science and engineering in the same way that scientists and engineers do. They give students specific ideas to consider when learning about a new topic. These ideas are intended to help students understand the topics at a deeper level.

In addition to supporting core ideas, the seven crosscutting concepts support one another. They are listed below with descriptions of their importance for all upper elementary students.

Patterns Recognizing patterns helps students sort and classify objects, describe rates of change and cycles, and make predictions.

Cause and Effect In their investigations, students observe patterns and then identify and test how two events may or may not be related.

Scale, Proportion, and Quantity Students recognize that objects and systems vary greatly in size and learn to measure using standard units.

Systems and System Models Describing and modeling systems helps students understand complex phenomena in terms of parts and their interactions.

Energy and Matter Students learn that matter is made of particles, that energy is transferred between objects, and that matter is neither lost nor gained when it changes.

Structure and Function Students explore identifying the smaller structures within larger ones and the functions of these structures.

Stability and Change Recognizing that change occurs at different rates helps students understand systems.

Each lesson is carefully developed to explain and integrate the crosscutting concept with core ideas.

While learning about the crosscutting concept Systems and System Models, students will discover how to describe a system using its components and interactions.

Connections to Engineering, Technology, and Applications of Science

The Next Generation Science Standards address engineering design as a process similar to, and just as important as, scientific inquiry. Engineering design is divided into three broad steps, each of which encompasses several of the science and engineering practices.

The steps are described by the grades 3–5 engineering design performance expectations, listed below.

- *3-5-ETS1-1. Define a simple design problem reflecting a need or want that includes specified criteria for success and constraints on materials, time, or cost.*

- *3-5-ETS1-2. Generate and compare multiple possible solutions to a problem based on how well each is likely to meet the criteria and constraints of the problem.*

- *3-5-ETS1-3. Plan and carry out fair tests in which variables are controlled and failure points are considered to identify aspects of a model or prototype that can be improved.*

Bring Science Alive! provides many opportunities for students to understand the work of engineers and use the engineering design process to solve problems relevant to the scientific knowledge they are simultaneously developing.

Engineering, Technology, and Applications of Science in the Investigations

When students study magnetic force in Unit 2, they learn how engineers use what they know about the properties of magnets to design and test trains that float above their tracks.

Engineering, Technology, and Applications of Science in the Student Text

Interactions of Science, Technology, Society and the Environment in the Student Text

While learning about the life cycles of plants, students read how scientists rely on technology such as climbing gear and zip lines to help them answer questions about rainforest plants.

Connections to the Nature of Science

The science and engineering practices describe how to engage in scientific inquiry. The disciplinary core ideas describe existing scientific knowledge. The crosscutting concepts provide a framework for connecting scientific knowledge. Students integrate these dimensions of learning when they learn what kinds of knowledge are scientific, how scientists develop that knowledge, and about the wide spectrum of people who engage in science.

Nature of Science in the Student Text

One of the basic understandings about the nature of science described in NGSS is that investigations use different tools, procedures, and techniques.

Nature of Science in the Investigations

How to Use This Program

1 The teacher begins each lesson with a **Presentation** that facilitates the lesson and the investigation.

2 In the Presentations, students participate in a hands-on **investigation** that blends the core ideas, science practices, and crosscutting concepts of NGSS.

3a In the online **Student Subscription**, students expand their knowledge through reading the Student Text, completing an Interactive Tutorial, and processing what they've learned in the **Interactive Student Notebook**.

3b Alternatively, students can read from the **Student Edition** and complete a consumable Interactive Student Notebook.

4 The lesson ends with students demonstrating their knowledge of each core idea, science practice, and crosscutting concept through a variety of paper and online **assessments**.

Literacy in Science

The Next Generation Science Standards were developed to work in tandem with the Common Core State Standards to ensure that students develop literacy skills through learning science. *Bring Science Alive!* builds on this synergy by emphasizing reading, writing, speaking and listening, and language skills while guiding students in developing their science knowledge.

Key Points from the ELA Common Core	*Bring Science Alive!*
Reading	
Informational and literary texts are balanced with at least 50% of reading time devoted to expository texts.	CCSS changes the emphasis in reading from being based primarily on literary texts to being balanced between literary and informational texts. *Bring Science Alive!* reflects this balance in its text. Each lesson has several sections of purely informational text that explains the content of that lesson. Each lesson is followed by a Reading Further, which blends literary and informational style text to engage students with the content even further.
Establishes a "staircase" of increasing complexity in what students must be able to read as they move throughout the grades.	*Bring Science Alive!* is written with close attention paid to the text complexity to make sure it fits into the "staircase" of increasingly sophisticated text that students should read as they progress through the grades. However, within each grade's text, there is variation in the complexity to ensure that there is challenging text for all students.
Emphasizes the close reading of text to determine main ideas, supporting details, and evidence.	The digital Interactive Tutorials encourage close reading of the text. They require students to answer questions using evidence from the text. Answering the questions requires a clear understanding of the main ideas and other details provided in the section.
Writing	
Three types of writing are emphasized from the earliest grades—writing to persuade, writing to inform/explain, and writing to convey experience.	NGSS and *Bring Science Alive!* require students to use all three types of writing emphasized by CCSS. In the investigations, students are often asked to construct written arguments to persuade their classmates of their explanation of a scientific concept. They also write accounts of their experiences in these activities and investigations, describing details of the experiment or design process. In the Interactive Student Notebook, students write explanations to demonstrate their understanding of the scientific concepts described in the text.
Effective use of evidence is central throughout the writing standards.	In all three types of writing, students are expected to use evidence appropriately to support their claims. They are given support in identifying key details which will serve most effectively as evidence. They also reflect on their use of evidence in various contexts to build an explicit understanding of the role evidence plays in science and argument in general.
Routine production of writing appropriate for a range of tasks, purposes, and audiences is emphasized.	Students routinely write in all of *Bring Science Alive!*'s curricula. The program emphasizes the flexibility and usefulness of writing to accomplish a variety of assignments. It also gives students exposure to the different expectations in writing for different purposes and audiences.

Key Points from the ELA Common Core	*Bring Science Alive!*

Speaking and Listening

Participation in rich, structured academic conversations in one-on-one, small-group, and whole class situations is emphasized in the standards.	Classrooms using *Bring Science Alive!* will regularly have structured science talks in which students reflect on their experiences and understanding of the investigations. They will also have regular discussions in smaller groups, ranging from discussions with a partner to groups of four or five students. These discussions are designed to build clear communication skills that are critical to success in science and all other fields of study.
Contributing accurate, relevant information; responding to and building on what others have said; and making comparisons and contrasts are important skills for productive conversations.	In all discussions, students are given support to help them learn to contribute relevant and accurate details and evidence. The cooperative tolerant classroom conventions emphasized throughout all of TCI's curricula encourage students to respond to and build on ideas and arguments presented by other students. *Bring Science Alive!* uses NGSS's crosscutting concepts to help students to compare and contrast relevant experiences across domains of science in discussions.

Language

Demonstrate command of the conventions of English when writing and speaking.	Throughout all the components of *Bring Science Alive!* students are expected to demonstrate command of the conventions of written and spoken English.
Acquire and use general academic and domain-specific words.	*Bring Science Alive!* has a progression of increasingly sophisticated vocabulary built into it with complexity suggested by the language used in NGSS. It is designed to emphasize key words used throughout a lesson or unit of study without overwhelming students with too many unfamiliar words. Every component of *Bring Science Alive!* makes use of the vocabulary and includes activities to help solidify comprehension.
Focus on developing skills to determine or clarify the meaning of unknown words or phrases.	Other science-related words which may be unfamiliar to students, but do not play a key role in the overall understanding of a concept, are put in italics and defined in context. This gives students ample opportunity and support in determining and clarifying the meaning of unfamiliar words using clues from the text.

Considerate Text

Sample Graphic Organizer

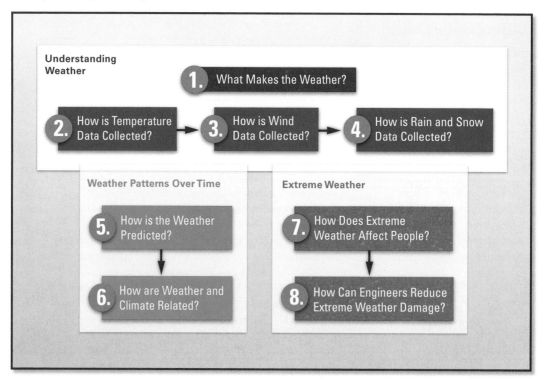

You are about to discover that *Bring Science Alive!* is both interesting and easy to understand. That's because our authors wrote it as a "considerate text," which is another way of saying that it makes readers want to read it. Here are some ways this book is considerate for all levels of readers:

- Each unit is carefully mapped out so that one lesson builds on the next. So, you will find a clear graphic organizer, like the one above, in each unit opener. The graphic organizer shows how all the lessons in the unit relate to one another. A **purple** lesson is the main idea, **blue** stands for lessons that support the main idea, and **green** and **red** lessons take those ideas even further.

- Short lessons make it easier for you to understand and remember what each one is about.

- Each section has a subtitle that provides an outline for your reading and is written with a clear focus. Information is presented in easy-to-manage chunks for better understanding.

- Important new words are in bold type. These words are defined in the glossary in the back of the book.

- Photos, illustrations, and diagrams provide additional information about the topic on the page.

How To Read the Table of Contents

The **lesson title** is also the lesson's Essential Question.

Each lesson has a **crosscutting concept** or 'theme' associated with it.

The **unit name** tells you the overall topic of the unit.

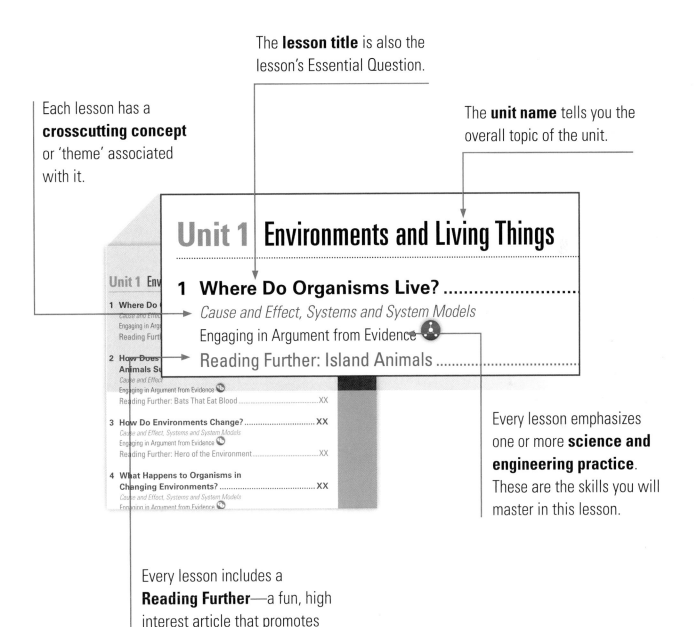

Every lesson emphasizes one or more **science and engineering practice**. These are the skills you will master in this lesson.

Every lesson includes a **Reading Further**—a fun, high interest article that promotes literacy and helps students engage with the content even further.

Contents

Unit 1 Environments and Living Things

Unit 2 Forces and Motion

Unit 3 Weather and Climate

Unit 4 Life Cycles and Traits

Environments and Living Things

What would it be like to dive into the ocean and observe the living things found there? You might see some fish swimming in a huge group. The group moves together, almost like a single fish. In this unit, you will discover how fishes and other living things survive in the place where they live. You will also find out what happens when the place where they live changes.

Unit Contents

Unit 1 Overview

Graphic Organizer: This unit is structured to teach how organisms and their environments interact using evidence from organisms and environments in the **present** and from fossils from the **past**.

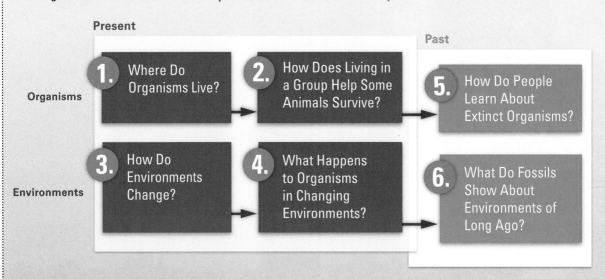

Present

Past

Organisms

1. Where Do Organisms Live?

2. How Does Living in a Group Help Some Animals Survive?

5. How Do People Learn About Extinct Organisms?

3. How Do Environments Change?

4. What Happens to Organisms in Changing Environments?

6. What Do Fossils Show About Environments of Long Ago?

Environments

NGSS Next Generation Science Standards

Performance Expectations

- 3-LS2-1. Construct an argument that some animals form groups that help members survive.

- 3-LS4-1. Analyze and interpret data from fossils to provide evidence of the organisms and the environments in which they lived long ago.

- 3-LS4-3. Construct an argument with evidence that in a particular habitat some organisms can survive well, some survive less well, and some cannot survive at all.

- 3-LS4-4. Make a claim about the merit of a solution to a problem caused when the environment changes and the types of plants and animals that live there may change.

Disciplinary Core Ideas

LS2.C: Ecosystem Dynamics, Functioning, and Resilience

- When the environment changes in ways that affect a place's physical characteristics, temperature, or availability of resources, some organisms survive and reproduce, others move to new locations, yet others move into the transformed environment, and some die.

LS2.D: Social Interactions and Group Behavior

- Being part of a group helps animals obtain food, defend themselves, and cope with changes. Groups may serve different functions and vary dramatically in size.

LS4.A: Evidence of Common Ancestry and Diversity

- Some kinds of plants and animals that once lived on Earth are no longer found anywhere.

- Fossils provide evidence about the types of organisms that lived long ago and also about the nature of their environments.

LS4.C: Adaptation

- For any particular environment, some kinds of organisms survive well, some survive less well, and some cannot survive at all.

LS4.D: Biodiversity and Humans

- Populations live in a variety of habitats, and change in those habitats affects the organisms living there.

Crosscutting Concepts

Cause and Effect

- Cause and effect relationships are routinely identified and used to explain change.

Scale, Proportion, and Quantity

- Observable phenomena exist from very short to very long time periods.

Systems and System Models

- A system can be described in terms of its components and their interactions.

 **Analyzing and Interpreting Data**

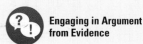 **Engaging in Argument from Evidence**

Have you ever wondered...

The living and nonliving things that surround a plant or animal are important to it. They can affect how well the plant or animal survives. This unit will help you answer these questions about plant and animal survival and many others you may ask.

What can a fossil show about an animal that lived long ago?

What do animals that live in the ocean eat?

What happened to all the large dinosaurs?

Where Do Organisms Live?

Science Vocabulary

bacteria

environment

organism

rainforest

Why do deer live in forests and fields? Organisms live where they can meet their needs. A deer can meet its needs in a forest. Some organisms live in a rainforest, where it is wet and hot. Others live underwater in a coral reef. Changes in their homes can cause the kinds of organisms that live there to change, too.

NGSS 3-LS4-3. Construct an argument with evidence that in a particular habitat some organisms can survive well, some survive less well, and some cannot survive at all.
3-LS4-4. Make a claim about the merit of a solution to a problem caused when the environment changes and the types of plants and animals that live there may change.

LS4.C. For any particular environment, some kinds of organisms survive well, some survive less well, and some cannot survive at all.
LS4.D. Populations live in a variety of habitats, and change in those habitats affects the organisms living there.

Cause and Effect Cause and effect relationships are routinely identified and used to explain change.
Systems and System Models A system can be described in terms of its components and their interactions.

 Engaging in Argument from Evidence

1. Types of Organisms

It's picnic time at a park. Lots of people and dogs sit on the grass. Birds are flying over the trees, and ants begin to crawl onto your blanket.

A living thing is called an **organism**. Grass, trees, people, dogs, birds, and ants are all organisms. There are many different kinds of organisms. Many of them that you see in the park are either plants or animals.

Some organisms are not plants or animals. For example, you might see mushrooms growing from a dead branch. The mushrooms are part of a *fungus* that lives in the wood. Many kinds of fungus grow on dead things and eat them. Bacteria live here, too. **Bacteria** are a type of tiny organism that cannot be seen without a microscope. Bacteria live all around you. Some kinds even live inside you. Many bacteria are helpful, while others can make you sick.

Another name for a living thing is organism. Both this tree branch and the mushrooms growing on it are parts of organisms.

2. Organisms and Their Environments

Many things can be found in a park. Some of them are organisms, while others are not living and have never been alive. Try to think of something in a park that is not living.

Living and Nonliving Things

Did you think of objects like rocks, water, or sand? None of these are alive. Sunlight and air are nonliving, too. A park contains both living and nonliving things. The park is an *environment* for the many organisms that live there. An **environment** is all the living and nonliving things that surround an organism.

Each kind of environment has certain features. For example, deserts are very dry and most are hot. Desert snakes and rabbits rest in the shade or underground when it is very hot. They have to be able to live with very little water.

A desert is a very dry environment. This snake searches very hard to find enough food and water.

Organisms Have Needs

Organisms need certain things to live. They must have water and enough food or sunlight. Their environment has to be the right temperature.

Living things depend on both living and nonliving parts of their environment. Living things in an environment depend on each other. For example, a squirrel might eat acorns that grow on an oak tree. It also builds its nest in the tree.

The oak tree also needs things from the environment. It needs nonliving things like rich soil, light, and water. It even needs the squirrel to help plant new oak trees with its acorns. If the environment changes, the organisms that live there can change.

Many types of oak tree cannot live in the desert because the desert environment is too dry and hot. The oak's needs cannot be met in a desert.

This oak tree meets its needs in this moist environment. It could not survive in a desert.

Plants in rainforests provide food and places to live for many different organisms.

3. Rainforest Environments

Monkeys swing from tree to tree using their long arms and tails. Many kinds of birds and insects fly overhead. Only a few plants live in the deep shade, but many ants do. *Fungi*, which means more than one fungus, and bacteria live on the forest floor. This is one type of *rainforest*.

A **rainforest** is a forest environment that gets a very large amount of rain. Tropical rainforests are hot and wet. Other rainforests are cooler, but just as wet. Many kinds of organisms live in rainforests.

Each organism in the rainforest depends on its environment. Monkeys need trees that grow close together. They can swing from tree to tree gathering fruits. Because the trees provide so much food, many animals never leave them. Birds build nests in trees. There, they eat fruits and insects.

These army ants live in the rainforest. They eat earthworms, spiders, and other animals that they can find.

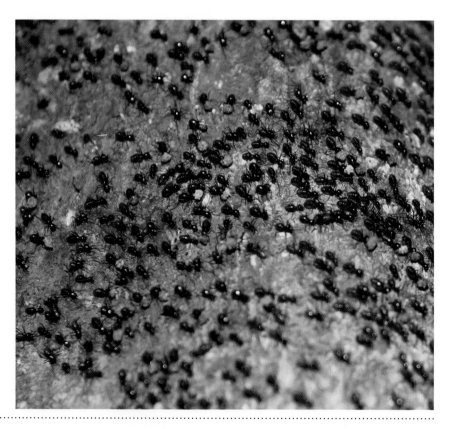

4. Coral Reef Environments

Suppose you are swimming in a warm ocean. Below, you see a bright and colorful structure. Lots of fish are swimming around. This is a coral reef.

Corals are tiny animals that build large rocky structures called *reefs*. Reefs are home to thousands of kinds of animals. Fish, sea stars, sea snails, and crabs are just a few. In fact, coral reefs are often called rainforests of the ocean because they are home to so many kinds of organisms.

The organisms here all depend on different parts of the reef for food and shelter. The coral needs the sunlight that enters the clear water. Some fish depend on the coral for food. The rocky reef protects small animals that hide in its cracks. Crabs hide there and come out to eat when it is safe. Sea turtles eat jellyfish. And sharks eat just about everything!

This is a coral reef in the warm waters of the Red Sea. Many different organisms meet their needs here.

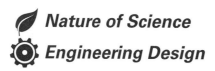

5. People Can Build Environments

Suppose a group of people wants to build an artificial coral reef. This reef would help many reef animals. What plans would they have to make?

Scientists and engineers often work in teams. The scientists first do research. They find out how natural coral reefs work. They learn what organisms live there and what their needs are. They find out what part of the reef environment each animal depends on to meet its needs.

The engineers use what scientists have learned to make decisions. They decide which places the reef could go. Engineers try out different materials that the reef could be built out of. They need to find a material that coral likes to grow on. They need to make sure the water conditions are right. Based on their decisions, they design the coral reef structure and then build it.

Engineers build artificial coral reefs. These structures help coral grow, which provides homes for other reef organisms.

Where Do Organisms Live?

1. Types of Organisms   All living things are organisms. Plants and animals are two types of organisms. But there are others, too, like fungi and bacteria. But bacteria are so tiny, they cannot be seen without a microscope.

2. Organisms and Their Environments   An organism's environment is all the living and nonliving things that surround it. An organism must meet its needs in its environment to survive. Many organisms cannot survive in different environments.

3. Rainforest Environments   A rainforest is a forest environment that is very wet. Some rainforests are hot and wet, and others are cooler and wet. Many organisms meet their needs in a rainforest.

4. Coral Reef Environments   Coral reefs are colorful ocean environments. Tiny organisms called corals build these environments in shallow tropical waters. Many organisms live in these environments and meet their needs there.

5. People Can Build Environments   Scientists and engineers work together to build artificial coral reefs. Scientists study how environments work and the organisms that live there. Then engineers can design structures that work as a new environment for those organisms.

Island Animals

Unusual organisms live on a group of islands in the Pacific Ocean. People visit just to see how the islands meet these organisms' needs.

The Captain tells you to prepare for landing. Looking out the plane window, you see a chain of small islands in the vast ocean. You have arrived at the Galápagos Islands!

The Galápagos Islands are located about 1,000 km (600 mi) off the coast of South America, near the equator. These islands are home to some animals not found anywhere else on Earth.

Once you land, head to the rocky ocean shores. Galápagos Penguins are smaller than penguins that live near the South Pole. You might see them waddling across the sand before hopping into the ocean. They spend most of their day in the cold water hunting for fish and staying cool in their warm environment.

Hurry! It's time to find the next island animal!

The Galápagos Islands lie off the coast of South America. Galápagos Penguins live on the shore and in the cool water.

Swimming Lizards

At another beach, you might see hundreds of scary-looking lizards lounging on the warm rocks. Some crawl off the rocks into the ocean. You could grab your snorkel and go for a swim with these lizards! Marine iguanas are the only lizards in the world that swim in the ocean.

A huge iguana with large claws and sharp teeth may look scary. But don't worry. They only eat plants. You will not see many plants on the rocky beaches where they live. So, marine iguanas dive into the ocean to eat seaweed.

You might feel chilly after snorkeling in the cold ocean. So do the lizards! They sunbathe on the beach to warm up after a swim. You might also see a basking iguana sneeze. Sneezing helps them get rid of extra salt they take in while they swim.

It is time to go! You still need to see the most famous animal in the Galápagos Islands!

Marine iguanas have flat tails that they use to swim. They warm up on the beach after a swim.

Galápagos tortoises live in grassy areas and can weigh up to 225 kg (500 lbs).

Giant Tortoises

You are knee deep in green grass when a large rock seems to move. That is not a rock! It is a giant tortoise! These tortoises are huge compared to other types of tortoises on Earth.

You will not see the Galápagos tortoises swimming. They live on land and spend their day eating, lying in the sun, and sleeping. They eat plant parts such as leaves, flowers, and fruit. Tortoises will eat almost any plant they can find.

These big tortoises need plenty of food. Some weigh more than 225 kg (about 500 lbs)!

Galápagos tortoises have an interesting way to survive. Their bodies are very good at storing water and food. Because of this, these tortoises can live for up to a year without eating!

Raising Tortoises

On your last stop, you visit a building with baby tortoises crawling all around! You are at the Charles Darwin Research Station. Scientists there hatch tortoise eggs and raise the babies. The research station creates a safe environment that has everything the young tortoises need. When the babies are older, they are released into the wild.

Scientists are raising baby tortoises because the wild tortoises face many threats. So do the other island animals. Before people came to the Galápagos Islands, there were not many threats to the animals. But people brought cats, dogs, and rats to the islands. These animals eat young penguins, marine iguanas, and baby tortoises. Even tourists can harm the environment on the islands. So, be cautious on your next adventure!

Scientists at the Charles Darwin Research Station raise baby tortoises and release them into the wild.

LESSON 2

How Does Living in a Group Help Some Animals Survive?

Science Vocabulary

prey

social animal

Why do you think these fish live in groups? Living in groups helps these animals survive more easily. It can help protect them against predators, like this shark. But not all animals live in groups. Some survive better if they live alone.

NGSS | **3-LS2-1.** Construct an argument that some animals form groups that help members survive.

LS2.D. Being part of a group helps animals obtain food, defend themselves, and cope with changes. Groups may serve different functions and vary dramatically in size.

Cause and Effect Cause and effect relationships are routinely identified and used to explain change.

 Engaging in Argument from Evidence

1. Some Kinds of Animals Live in Groups

In nature, many animals like lions or honeybees live in groups. Living in groups helps these animals meet their needs.

Lions and honeybees are *social animals*. **Social animals** are animals of the same kind that live in a group to meet their needs. The members of the group interact with each other to survive.

The size of an animal group can vary. Some are very small. Others are very large. Small groups, like lion prides, might have just five or six members. Large groups, like honeybee hives, might have many thousands. Other groups have millions!

Social animals form groups for different reasons. Some do it for protection. Others do it to find food or raise young. Others do it to help members cope with changes in the environment.

Honeybees live in very large groups.

Lions are social animals. A pride of lions may include one or more males, several females, and their cubs.

This male rooster is ready to protect the female hen looking for food in the grass.

2. The Benefits of Living in Groups

In a group of animals, different members have different jobs. For example, elephants often form groups. Some of the big adult elephants guard the herd against predators. Others may look for food. Some may take care of the young elephants.

Group Members Defend the Group

Living in a group can help an animal survive. Each animal in a group has a role to play. When each member does its job, it helps the whole group. Members of a group often work together to stay safe from animals that want to eat them. Group members protect the babies in the group. They also protect those that are sick or hurt. In some groups, one animal may be in charge. This animal helps to prevent fighting. Roosters, for example, protect female chickens. They guard them while the chickens look for food or raise young.

The larger elephants in this group form a ring on the outside to protect the small, young ones on the inside. Protection is one benefit of living in a group.

Group Members Obtain Food

The job of some group members is to find food. Female lions hunt together and share the food they catch with other pride members. It is easier for several lions to hunt together for food than for one lion to hunt alone. Killer whales also hunt in groups and share the food they catch.

Killer whales hunt together to catch porpoises, seals and even large whales. The killer whales all get to share this food.

Group Members Care for Young

Female lions in a pride often have their cubs at about the same time. They care for the cubs together. Elephants also care for their young together.

Group Members Cope with Changes

When the weather turns cold in autumn, many birds, such as geese, form groups that fly south for winter. Other birds form groups that help them find food and mates, stay warm, and keep safe. Penguins, for example, get together when it is cold.

Leopards hunt alone so that they can sneak up on prey. Often, they drag their prey into a tree so they can eat safely.

3. Some Kinds of Animals Live Alone

Leopards are large cats, like lions. But leopards do not live in groups. Why do some kinds of animals live alone?

An animal that is hunted and eaten is called **prey**. Lions live in open places where they can be easily seen by their prey. A group of lions can more easily surround and kill its prey than a single lion can. Lions survive well by living in a group.

Leopards use a different hunting style. The places where they live have more trees for cover. A single leopard needs to catch less food than a group of lions do. Leopards hunt by sneaking up on prey. Then they chase it and pounce. They drag their prey up into a tree where they can eat it safely. A leopard survives better when it is alone. By hunting alone, the prey will not see a leopard coming. And it does not have to share the food.

How Does Living in a Group Help Some Animals Survive?

1. Some Kinds of Animals Live in Groups   Some animals are social animals, which means they like to live near other animals of their same kind. Different kinds of animals form groups of different sizes. Living in groups benefits animals in different ways.

2. The Benefits of Living in Groups   Animals that live in groups do so because it helps them survive. Some members protect the group. Others might look for food while some care for or protect the young. Groups can also help animals adjust to changes in their environment.

3. Some Kinds of Animals Live Alone   Not all animals live in groups. Some benefit more from living alone. This helps some animals to hunt their prey while hidden. Types of animals that live alone do not have to share their food either.

Bats That Eat Blood

Just mentioning a vampire bat is enough to scare some people. But these bats are not so scary when you learn more about them. They take very good care of one another.

The innocent victim sleeps soundly, unaware of what lurks nearby in the night. Suddenly, a dark figure hops onto its back. Sharp teeth slash through skin. Blood flows from the wound. The hungry vampire licks up its meal and then flies away with a full belly. Is this a scene from a monster movie?

This is no movie—it happens in real life! Vampire bats are real animals, and they do drink blood. But they are not like the scary monster seen in movies. Vampire bats are small animals. They are smaller than robins. They live in places like Mexico where it is very warm all year long. There, they like to feed on cows, horses, and wild animals—not people. The small amount of blood they drink is not even enough to harm their dinner host.

Vampire bats do not have many teeth because they do not chew their food. But the teeth they do have are very sharp.

Sharing a Meal

Unlike many scary-movie monsters, vampire bats are not loners. They live with other bats in groups called colonies. During the day, vampire bats nestle together in dark places, like a cave or hollow tree.

Living in groups solves another big problem. A vampire bat has only one meal a night. Two or three nights without eating and it will starve. Luckily, other bats will share their food.

How does a bat get another bat to share? Vampire bats rarely share their meals with strangers. To ask for a meal, a hungry bat will groom its neighbor. In return, the neighbor throws up some blood for the hungry bat to eat. It may sound unpleasant, but the bats do not mind. The shared meal keeps them alive.

Vampire bats live in colonies to keep warm and to share food. They hang upside down when they sleep.

Caring for Pups

Vampire bats take care of each other in other ways, too. They groom each other even when they are not hungry. In fact, mother bats keep their young babies very tidy.

Vampire bat mothers also feed their babies, which are called pups. A pup holds tight to its mother as she flies through the night in search of food. But pups do not drink blood when they are first born. They drink their mother's milk. When the baby is about a month old, its mother will start to throw up blood for it to eat. When it is a little older, it learns to hunt with its mother.

Young bats do not always leave home once they know how to hunt. Living together in a group helps the pups. If something happens to a mother, her pup may be adopted by another female bat.

Vampire bat pups depend on their mothers for months.

A medicine made from vampire bat saliva may help people. It can help people who have had a stroke.

Medicine from Bat Saliva

Vampire bats are not really like the monsters in scary movies. But they can cause problems for real life farm animals. They may spread diseases, such as rabies, when they feed.

One good thing has come from studying vampire bats. It turns out that their saliva is special. It stops scabs from forming. Scabs form to stop bleeding. However, the bites made by vampire bats keep bleeding because of the bat saliva. This lets the bats feed longer.

Scientists have used what they learned about bat saliva to make a new medicine. It may help people who have had a stroke. Strokes can be caused by blood clots in the brain. The medicine breaks up the clots and may save lives. Knowing how harmless, and even helpful, vampire bats can be makes being scared of them seem a little batty.

How Do Environments Change?

Science Vocabulary

natural resource

species

How do you think this forest environment has changed? Sometimes, environments change because of natural causes, like wildfires and volcanoes. When an environment changes, the living and nonliving members of the environment can also change.

NGSS

3-LS4-3. Construct an argument with evidence that in a particular habitat some organisms can survive well, some survive less well, and some cannot survive at all.
3-LS4-4. Make a claim about the merit of a solution to a problem caused when the environment changes and the types of plants and animals that live there may change.

LS2.C. When the environment changes in ways that affect a place's physical characteristics, temperature, or availability of resources, some organisms survive and reproduce, others move to new locations, yet others move into the transformed environment, and some die.
LS4.C. For any particular environment, some kinds of organisms survive well, some survive less well, and some cannot survive at all.
LS4.D. Populations live in a variety of habitats, and change in those habitats affects the organisms living there.

Cause and Effect Cause and effect relationships are routinely identified and used to explain change.
Systems and System Models A system can be described in terms of its components and their interactions.

Engaging in Argument from Evidence

26   Unit 1 Environments and Living Things

1. Environments Can Change

You may have taken a long trip at some time. Did you notice any environments that looked strange? A forest may have looked burned or the water in a river may have looked muddy.

Many things can cause an environment to change. Natural events, such as an increase or decrease in rainfall, can cause change. Other changes can be caused by humans. Humans may cut down part of a forest to build a road. Some changes are fast and happen within days or minutes. Others are slow and take years to happen.

When a change in an environment occurs, it affects the *species* that live there. A **species** is a group of living things of the same kind. Leopards make up one species, while lions make up another. Each kind of plant is a separate species. Species may move into or out of changing environments.

Part of this forest has been burned by a forest fire. Forest fires are one event that can change forest environments.

The Grand Canyon formed when water and wind wore away the rock. The environment changed over millions of years.

Water once flowed in this river bed, but the water is now gone. The environment changed as the water dried up.

2. Slow Environmental Changes

Have you ever visited the Grand Canyon or seen an image of it? Do you think it always looked like this, or has it changed?

Rock Wears Away

Rock and soil can be worn away by wind and water. These effects are usually very slow. Over long periods of time they change the way an environment looks. The Grand Canyon formed in this way. Over millions of years, the river wore down the rock and then carried it away.

Changes in Temperature or Rainfall

Changes in temperature or rainfall can change an area. It may take many years for these changes to occur. Fish and other water animals can die if rivers dry up. Plants cannot live if their soil dries out. This causes the animals that eat the plants to die or move away. A change in temperature or in the amount of rain can change an area over time.

This is a large mine that people have created to remove metals from the earth. Creating this mine changed the original environment.

Resource Removal

A **natural resource** is a useful material that comes from the environment. Water is a natural resource you use. Trees, metals, and air are too.

Humans use a lot of Earth's resources to meet their needs and wants. Many, such as metals, can never be replaced when they are used up. Other resources, such as trees, take time to regrow. The environment changes when a resource is gone.

Invasive Species

Sometimes humans move a species to an area where it did not live before. If the organism causes problems in the new environment, it is called an *invasive species*. It may grow faster or have fewer enemies than the native species that live there. Over time, an invasive species can crowd out local plants and animals. They may not be able to live in this area anymore.

Iceplants are an invasive species in California.

This forest was flooded. Floods like this one can change environments by destroying organisms and by moving soil.

3. Fast Environmental Changes

During a storm, lightning may strike a tree in a forest. The tree starts to burn. How does a forest fire change an environment?

Wildfires and Floods

Not all changes to an environment take years to happen. Some natural events can cause change within days, or even within minutes. A burning tree can spread fire quickly to nearby trees. Wildfires can kill many plants. Animals that eat the plants might have no food to eat. A wildfire can cause a forest environment to change quickly.

A flood happens when heavy rain causes a body of water such as a river to overflow onto dry land. Floods can wash away soil and kill the plants that grow in the area. They can damage or destroy buildings and roads. After a flood, new plants and animals move in, and the environment changes.

Earthquakes, Landslides, and Volcanic Eruptions

An earthquake causes the ground to shake suddenly. It can cause the land to shift or make huge waves in the ocean. Earthquakes cause landslides when rocks and soil on a hillside shake loose and slide down. Heavy rain also causes landslides when mud gets slippery and slides downhill. Landslides and earthquakes change environments very quickly.

When a volcano erupts, changes in the environment occur in minutes or days. Soil is covered with melted rock or ashes. When the melted rock cools and hardens, Earth's surface has changed. The volcano's shape may have changed. Plants cannot grow right away when soil is covered by volcanos. And animals cannot live without plants to eat.

Landslides like this can be caused by earthquakes or heavy rainfall.

As volcanos erupt, they change the environment around them very quickly.

Engineering Design

4. Engineers Can Change Environments

Some rivers flood almost every spring. Heavy rain causes them to overflow. Humans can solve this problem, but new problems will arise.

Building a dam across a river can prevent floods. The dam holds water behind it to form a lake. Engineers can adjust the dam's gates. They let water out of the lake slowly. This way it does not flood and people downstream can use it all year.

But building a dam changes the environment. Scientists research what affect the dam will have on the environment. Plants and animal species may lose their homes. Scientists must research the needs of species that live near the river. Rare species should be preserved. Engineers must make use of science findings to make sure a dam can prevent floods without causing too many problems.

This dam changed the environment of the river quickly. It is important for scientists and engineers to research what dams will do before they build them.

How Do Environments Change?

1. Environments Can Change Environments can change for many different reasons. They can change due to natural events, or they can change because of humans. When environments change, those changes affect the species that live there.

2. Slow Environmental Changes Some things cause environments to change slowly. Rock can wear away, or the temperature and amount of rainfall can change over many years. When resources disappear or new species are introduced, environments can change slowly.

3. Fast Environmental Changes Other things cause environments to change quickly. Natural disasters, like earthquakes, landslides, and volcanoes cause fast changes. So do wildfires and floods. These changes also affect the organisms in that environment.

4. Engineers Can Change Environments Many human activities change environments, like building dams. Before engineers build a dam, they should research how that dam will affect the river environment. They need to make sure the dam will have the right effects.

Hero of the Environment

Changes in ocean environments affect the organisms that live there—
at times for the worse. But sometimes a hero steps in to save them.

There is a danger zone in the Gulf of Mexico the size of the state of New Jersey. All of the animals that were able to leave have already left. If they did not, they would die. But the ocean here was not always this way. It used to be full of life. What caused this environment to become so deadly?

Dr. Nancy Rabalais, Marine Ecologist

Like any good detective, Dr. Nancy Rabalais is trying to get to the bottom of this mystery. Dr. Rabalais is a marine ecologist, which means she studies the environment and organisms in the ocean. For about 30 years, Dr. Rabalais has been studying mysterious places called dead zones. In a dead zone, there is not enough oxygen in the water. So, fish and other creatures that live there cannot breathe.

Dr. Nancy Rabalais investigates dead zones in the Gulf of Mexico. She does much of her work on a boat called the *Pelican*.

What Causes the Dead Zone?

Dr. Rabalais has seen dead zones up close. In fact, she dives right into them! She and her team scuba dive to study the ocean environment.

Dr. Rabalais has worked with many scientists to discover the main cause of the dead zone—fertilizer. Farmers add fertilizer to land far away from the ocean. The fertilizer gets washed into rivers, which carry it into the Gulf. The fertilizer causes too much algae to grow in the ocean. When the algae die and rot, all of the oxygen in the water gets used up. This creates the dead zone.

Now that people know the cause of the dead zone, they are making changes to fix it. For example, some farmers are changing the way they farm so that less fertilizer enters the ocean. Maybe you can make changes to help protect the ocean environment. Then you could be a hero, too!

Dr. Rabalais scuba dives to investigate dead zones.

The Mississippi River carries materials, including fertilizer, into the Gulf of Mexico. The fertilizer and other farming materials cause the dead zone.

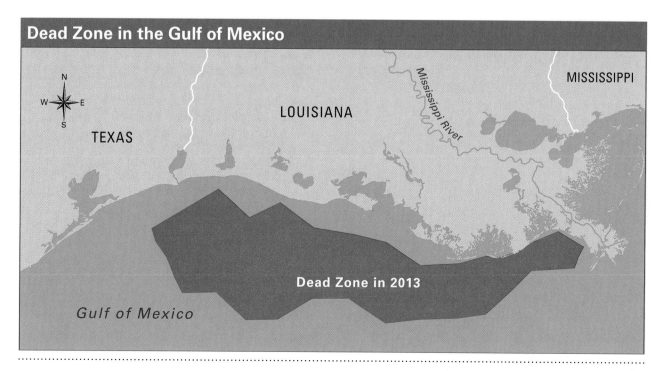

Dead Zone in the Gulf of Mexico

N W E S

MISSISSIPPI

LOUISIANA

Mississippi River

TEXAS

Dead Zone in 2013

Gulf of Mexico

LESSON 4

What Happens to Organisms in Changing Environments?

Science Vocabulary

adaptation
behavior
reproduce

Different species have different adaptations that help them survive in their environments. Sometimes their environments change, which can cause problems for the organisms that live in these environments. So, the organisms must change their behaviors or move to a new environment in order to survive.

NGSS

3-LS4-3. Construct an argument with evidence that in a particular habitat some organisms can survive well, some survive less well, and some cannot survive at all.
3-LS4-4. Make a claim about the merit of a solution to a problem caused when the environment changes and the types of plants and animals that live there may change.

LS2.C. When the environment changes in ways that affect a place's physical characteristics, temperature, or availability of resources, some organisms survive and reproduce, others move to new locations, yet others move into the transformed environment, and some die.
LS4.C. For any particular environment, some kinds of organisms survive well, some survive less well, and some cannot survive at all.
LS4.D. Populations live in a variety of habitats, and change in those habitats affects the organisms living there.

Cause and Effect Cause and effect relationships are routinely identified and used to explain change.
Systems and System Models A system can be described in terms of its components and their interactions.

 Engaging in Argument from Evidence

1. Species Have Adaptations

A leopard has fur with spots that help it hide among plants and sneak up on its prey. Sneaking up on prey alone is the leopard's hunting style. This hunting style helps it capture food.

A leopard's hunting style is a *behavior*. A **behavior** is an action that an organism does. The leopard's spotted fur is a body part. A behavior or body part that helps an organism survive and reproduce in its environment is called an **adaptation**. Leopards have sharp teeth for tearing meat. Sharp teeth are an adaptation. A leopard is well adapted to its forest environment. Its body parts and behaviors help it survive where it lives.

Lions are adapted to their environment of open grassland. They hunt in groups. They also have sharp teeth for tearing meat, but their fur has no spots. It blends in better with the grass where they live.

Leopards have long, sharp teeth for biting and tearing meat. Sharp teeth are an adaptation.

2. Some Organisms Adjust to Changing Environments

Suppose both green and brown beetles live in an area. Birds cannot easily see green beetles that hide on green plant leaves. What would happen if the leaves turned brown because the environment got much hotter?

Environments Change

You have read about the many ways an environment can change. After a change, some of the organisms that live there may not be as well adapted. They may die. A green beetle on a brown leaf would be seen and eaten by a bird. Now, a brown beetle has better adaptations. Its brown color is an adaptation that will help it survive in the new environment. Each type of beetle has different adaptations that help it survive and reproduce in different environments. To **reproduce** means to make more of the same kind of organism.

These beetles have different adaptations. Their adaptations help them survive in different environments.

Behaviors Help Animals Survive

When an area changes, some adaptations may not work anymore. But most organisms cannot change their body parts. Adult beetles that start out one color usually stay that color their whole lives. So most animals also use behaviors to survive.

A few organisms *can* change their bodies. Chameleons are a kind of lizard that can change the color of their skin. Some change their color when they see an animal that wants to eat them. One type of chameleon even turns one color if it sees a bird and a different color if it sees a snake! These behaviors help chameleons survive.

A small desert rat cannot change its body parts to adjust to the heat. But it can change its behavior. The rat digs a hole where it can hide during the hot day. Other animals can even learn new behaviors throughout their lives that help them survive.

Chameleons are lizards that can change the color of their skin. Some chameleons use this behavior to hide from animals that want to eat them.

This desert rat digs a burrow in the ground and hides during the heat of the day. This behavior helps it survive in the desert.

Plants with big leaves like these are adapted to live on the ground in the rainforest. If the trees that grow over them are cut down, these plants may not be able to survive in the changing environment.

3. Organisms in a Changing Rainforest

Humans are cutting down trees in the world's rainforests. When a rainforest changes, what happens to the species that live there?

Many rainforest species live and meet their needs only in one place. Cutting down even small areas of forest can take away the only home of some species. Many will die. Others move away. A few will survive and stay.

Cutting down trees increases the amount of light on the ground. Some plants are adapted to shade and too much light burns their leaves. They die, or do not grow well. Plants that like a lot of light may take their place. Cutting down trees also dries out the soil. Without roots to hold it in place, soil can be lost. As the environment changes, so do the species that live there. Some species die out or leave the environment while others move in.

4. Organisms in a Changing Coral Reef

Humans also change coral reef environments. Invasive species harm reefs and their organisms. So does too much fishing. Warm water and pollution also harm reefs.

Corals are adapted to water of a certain temperature. They are killed by water that is too warm. Fish and other sea animals that rely on corals for food will leave the reef. Some will start to eat new food and will survive and reproduce.

Many reef fish have mouths adapted for eating certain kinds of food. If that food dies, they have nothing to eat. Many reef fish also hide in the reef to escape danger. Their shape lets them make quick turns and stop. This way they avoid enemies. If the coral reef disappears, they will have nowhere to hide and nothing to eat. They might not be able to survive in the new environment.

The red lionfish shown here is an invasive species in some reefs. It has no enemies and eats many of the native fish on the reef. This changes the coral reef environment.

5. Some Organisms Move to New Environments

You may have seen bears eating out of trash cans on the news. But bears normally live in the woods and eat wild foods. Why do you think bears might start eating food out of trash cans?

When an environment changes, some organisms either move or stay and have to change. For example, suppose that humans bulldoze a forest. This would cause all of the bears that live in that forest and eat berries to have no food. They must either move to a new environment or stay and learn to eat something new. Otherwise they will die.

Does moving solve the problem of a changed environment? It might if an organism can find another home that meets its needs. But a lot of forests already have other bears. There is no room for new bears. Bears with nowhere to go might try to stay and change their behavior to eat new foods.

This bear is eating berries in the wild. In other places where their environments have been changed by humans, some bears have started eating human garbage.

What Happens to Organisms in Changing Environments?

1. Species Have Adaptations   Organisms have adaptations that help them survive in their environments. These adaptations can be body parts like sharp teeth or behaviors like knowing how to hunt.

2. Some Organisms Adjust to Changing Environments   When an environment changes, some organisms survive better than others. Most adaptations cannot be changed in an animal's lifetime, but some animals change their behaviors. This helps them survive during times of change.

3. Organisms in a Changing Rainforest   Humans are cutting down the world's rainforests. Many of the creatures there only live in one area. When a rainforest environment changes, the organisms that cannot move or adjust will die.

4. Organisms in a Changing Coral Reef   Humans are changing coral reefs. When a coral reef environment changes, organisms must move or adjust to the new environment. Organisms that cannot move or adjust will die.

5. Some Organisms Move to New Environments   When most organisms move to new environments, they must find one that is similar to their old environment. If there is no room in another environment, they must adjust to the changes in their current home. Otherwise they will die.

Road Safety for Wildlife

Even something as simple as a new road changes the environment and affects the animals that live there. But many animals can change their behaviors when people invent safer ways for animals to cross.

Watch out for that turtle in the road! Screech! Whew. We stopped in time. Why *did* the turtle cross the road? No joke—engineers want to know.

Even though it is dangerous, animals cross busy roads. Salamanders scurry across wet roads after an evening rain. Bears lumber across mountain highways. Turtles walk slowly and steadily to get to the other side.

Turtles, bears, and other animals cross roads that cut through their environments. Many animals are injured or killed this way.

Roads cut through the environments where these animals live. Salamanders cross roads to get to ponds. Bears need to find food. Turtles may be looking for a place to make a nest. So, engineers are now designing roads with animals in mind.

Passing Under and Over

In some places, animals do not have to walk on a road to cross it anymore. They can go under or pass over it!

In some areas, engineers have added animal tunnels and passageways under roads. Turtles, salamanders, and mountain goats have all learned to use them. They cross safely while cars zoom quickly overhead.

When designing a tunnel, engineers must think of the needs of the animals. Salamanders do not like a dry tunnel. So, engineers put holes in the top of salamander tunnels. Rain falls through the holes. This keeps the tunnels damp.

In other places, animals have a way to pass over the roadway. Engineers design bridges planted with grasses and trees. Bears and other animals safely walk over the traffic below.

This tunnel allows frogs to pass safely under the road instead of trying to hop across it.

An overpass lets bears and other animals stay off the highway.

Placing Tunnels

Once engineers have designed an animal passageway, where do they put it? For salamanders, the answer is clear.

In spring, salamanders move from their homes on the forest floor to pools of water. Every year, they cross the same stretches of road. So, each spring, volunteers come out when it is dark and wet. Wearing raincoats and carrying buckets, they collect the animals. Into the buckets they go for a safe ride across the road.

A place where salamanders cross the road every year is a very good place for a salamander tunnel. To find where other animals need a safe place to cross, scientists do research. They study the numbers and behaviors of the animals in an area. But there is still one thing the engineers need to think about.

Salamanders cross roads in the same places each year. These are the places scientists choose for tunnels.

Directing Animal Traffic

Signs and road markings let people know where to find a safe crosswalk. But other animals do not read. Engineers must use other ways to direct animal traffic to tunnels or bridges.

Sometimes engineers put tunnels or bridges near the paths animals are known to take. This makes it more likely that the animals will use them. At other times, they get rid of the old, well-traveled paths. Then, they make new paths that lead the animals to the new passageway.

Just making a new route is not always enough. Engineers sometimes have to block the old path. They build a small fence on either side of the opening meant for animals. Animals cannot cross the fence, so they use the new route instead. Whatever the reason animals cross the road, engineers make sure they do it safely!

Engineers use different methods to direct animal traffic to tunnels or bridges. Fences help direct animals to pass under the road.

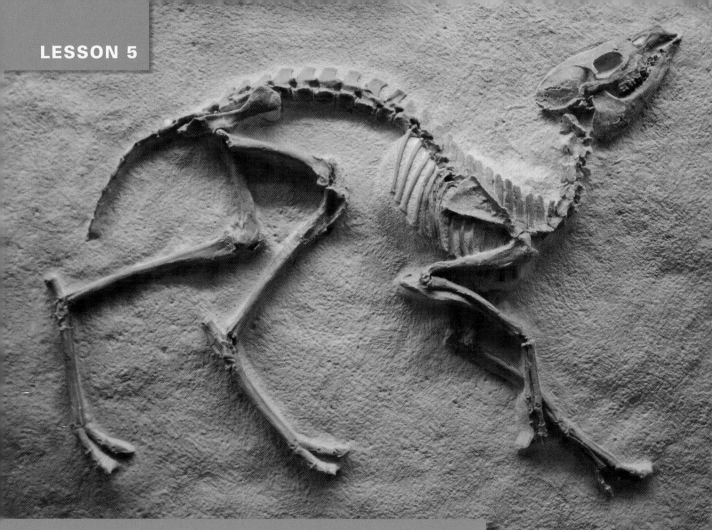

How Do People Learn About Extinct Organisms?

Science Vocabulary

endangered

extinct

fossil

Most organisms that have lived on Earth died a long time ago. How do scientists learn about them? They study fossils. There are many types of fossils, and scientists study them to learn about many extinct species, like dinosaurs. Scientists have learned what dinosaurs looked like and how they behaved.

NGSS

3-LS4-1. Analyze and interpret data from fossils to provide evidence of the organisms and the environments in which they lived long ago.

LS4.A. • Some kinds of plants and animals that once lived on Earth are no longer found anywhere. • Fossils provide evidence about the types of organisms that lived long ago and also about the nature of their environments.

Scale, Proportion, and Quantity Observable phenomena exist from very short to very long time periods.

Analyzing and Interpreting Data

1. Extinction

Have you ever seen a *Tyrannosaurus rex*? Of course not! These dinosaurs no longer exist. Millions of years ago, dinosaurs lived all over Earth. But a sudden change in their environment killed most of the dinosaurs.

The *T. rex* is *extinct*. An **extinct** species has no living members. Many kinds of plants and animals that once lived on Earth are now extinct. Organisms can go extinct very quickly. Every day, some species go extinct.

Some organisms start to die when their environment changes. When not many of them are left, their species is now called *endangered*. **Endangered** means they are in danger of going extinct. If the members of an endangered species keep dying faster than they reproduce, the species might go extinct.

Mountain gorillas are endangered, which means many of them are dying and their species is in danger of going extinct.

This is a *Tyrannosaurus rex* skeleton. All the large dinosaurs like the *T. rex* are extinct, which means there are no more alive on Earth.

These tracks were made by a dinosaur walking in mud. They have been preserved for millions of years.

2. Fossils

As you know, the large dinosaurs that used to roam Earth are now extinct. So, how do people know what dinosaurs looked like?

Some extinct species have left behind *fossils*. A **fossil** is the remaining pieces or trace of an organism that lived long ago. Most fossils come from hard body parts such as bones or shells. Some fossils are of small organisms, like insects. Others are of large organisms, like the *T. rex*. There are several kinds of fossils.

Trace Fossils

Trace fossils give hints about how an animal lived. Trace fossils are not actual body parts. Instead, they are clues about an organism. Dinosaur footprints are trace fossils. They show whether the animal used two legs or four. They show whether it walked or ran or hopped.

Mold and Cast Fossils

A *mold fossil* is a hollow space in a rock shaped like the organism part that formed it. Leaves, shells, or bones often fall into mud. Sometimes, the mud becomes rock. Now, even after the part of the organism rots away, the impression in the rock is still there.

Sometimes, the inside of the mold gets filled with rock. This makes a copy of the body part that made the mold. This type of fossil is called a *cast fossil*.

This cast fossil formed when an imprint of a shell formed a mold and filled with rock.

Whole Body Fossils

Sometimes fossils of a whole body are found. Some of these, especially fossils of insects, are found in a sticky tree substance called *resin*. As it dries, the resin turns into a hard substance called *amber*. These fossils form faster than most other types. But it still takes millions of years. The organism in the amber becomes a *whole body fossil*.

These ancient insects where trapped in tree resin and fossilized. This amber is an example of a whole body fossil.

When scientists find enough fossil bones, they can build skeletons like this one. They use the skeletons to learn about what the dinosaurs were like when they were alive.

3. Learning About Dinosaurs from Fossils

Dinosaurs left behind many fossils. We have learned a lot about these animals from their fossils.

Physical Features of Dinosaurs

Scientists have dug up fossils of many dinosaur species. They can look at the bones to learn about the dinosaurs. Large dinosaurs had large bones. Smaller dinosaurs had shorter bones. Some dinosaurs had wings and could fly like birds. Scientists have rebuilt skeletons using the bones they found.

Some kinds of dinosaurs had horns or spines. A few had bodies that were covered with thick armor. Fossils found in China show that many dinosaurs even had feathers!

Many fossil teeth have also been found. Many kinds of dinosaurs had flat teeth and ate plants. Sharp, pointed teeth show that other kinds of dinosaurs ate meat.

Behaviors of Dinosaurs

Fossil footprints show that some dinosaurs walked on four legs. Others had two legs and two short arms. Many dinosaur fossils are found in groups, which might show that they lived in families. Dinosaurs laid eggs with hard shells that were similar to bird eggs. Fossil dinosaur eggs have been found in nests. It seems likely that some dinosaur parents took care of their young.

Where and When Dinosaurs Lived

Dinosaur fossils have been found all around Earth. This tells us that they lived in many different environments. They also lived at many different times. The age of fossils can be measured. Scientists find that dinosaurs lived on Earth for almost 200 million years. These species went extinct about 65 million years ago.

Fossilized dinosaur eggs have been found in nests. This shows that dinosaurs, like many birds today, took care of their young.

4. Most Organisms Do Not Form Fossils

Many kinds of fossils have been found. You might even find fossils where you live. But actually, most organisms never form fossils at all.

Organisms with hard parts are most likely to form fossils. Often, only bones and teeth or a shell remain. The rest of the organism decays or is eaten. Worms and jellyfish have only soft body parts. These animals rarely form fossils, but a few fossils of soft parts have been found. They were frozen or preserved before they decayed.

To form a fossil, a dead organism must be buried quickly so that it will not decay or be eaten. Some places have more mud and sediments than others. Those places form more fossils than others. For example, animals that crawl on the bottom of the ocean form many fossils. Swimming creatures form fewer.

These are fossils of jellyfish. Since jellyfish are soft animals, this kind of fossil is very rare.

How Do People Learn About Extinct Organisms?

1. Extinction   When all the organisms of one species die, that species is extinct. Many kinds of plants and animals are now extinct. Some species go extinct every day. Before a species goes extinct, it is usually endangered, which means very few members are left alive. Many species on Earth today are endangered.

2. Fossils   Some extinct organisms leave fossils. Most fossils come from hard body parts like bones or shells. But some fossils are not of body parts. There are many different kinds of fossils. Some of the different kinds are trace fossils, mold fossils, cast fossils, and whole body fossils.

3. Learning About Dinosaurs from Fossils   Scientists learn about dinosaurs by studying their fossils. The fossils can show physical features like size. Sometimes they show the dinosaurs' behaviors. The fossils also show how long ago the dinosaurs lived and when they became extinct.

4. Most Organisms Do Not Form Fossils   Most organisms do not form fossils when they die. Soft parts rot very quickly and do not fossilize well. So fossils of organisms with soft bodies are very rare. If an organism is covered quickly after it dies, it is much more likely to form a fossil.

Everybody Loves *T. rex*

You have never seen huge ancient dinosaurs alive. Yet, you can still picture what they looked like. Fossils provide clues to how they looked. One is more famous than all the others.

Most people can name at least one dinosaur—*Tyrannosaurus rex*. This ancient celebrity is so famous, it has a nickname. Can you guess it? *T. rex*! The "king" of the dinosaurs has starred in movies. Children play with its image in toys. Everybody seems to love *T. rex*. But how much do people know about this popular beast?

T. rex actually roamed the Earth over 65 million years ago. If it were alive today, *T. rex* would tower over you. About eight of your classmates would need to lie in a line to be as long as *T. rex*! It was a hunter with powerful legs, huge jaws, and sharp teeth. Yet, its arms were very small.

T. rex is interesting to most people. No one has ever seen a living *T. rex* because the dinosaur went extinct millions of years ago.

Unearthing a Giant Skeleton

Scientists have such a good idea of what *T. rex* looked like because of the fossils people have found. Fossil hunter Barnum Brown found the first *T. rex* fossil more than 100 years ago. He was searching for fossils in Montana. He didn't know what he had found. But he knew it was going to be an exciting discovery. His team spent three years digging up the incredible fossil.

Brown packed up the gigantic skull, tiny arms, and all of the other parts he found. Then he sent them across the country by train to a museum in New York City. There, scientists carefully put all of the bones back together. How did they know how the bones fit together? They used what they knew about the skeletons of living animals. When they were done, the skeleton showed a creature unlike anything people had imagined before.

Barnum Brown was a fossil hunter who found many dinosaur fossils. He discovered the first fossil skeleton of *T. rex.*

Changing Postures

The interest in *T. rex* began when people saw the first skeleton. People then found more skeletons, some even bigger than the first. Scientists changed what they thought about *T. rex* when comparing these fossils. Still, many people would draw a picture of *T. rex* that looks like the first skeleton. And one part of their pictures would be wrong.

Fossils usually do not show how a dinosaur stood or walked. Scientists have to study the bones and consider how animals today stand and walk. The scientists who put the first *T. rex* skeleton together thought it stood up straight. They showed its tail dragging on the ground. But scientists have since learned that *T. rex* actually stood with its tail sticking out. Its back was horizontal.

Scientists first thought *T. rex* stood upright. And that is the way *T. rex* toys were made. Today, skeletons in museums show the actual way that *T. rex* stood.

More to Learn

Scientists are still studying *T. rex* fossils. And they still have many unanswered questions. One question is why such a huge dinosaur had such tiny arms. We know that the arms were not totally useless. Fossils show that strong muscles were attached to the arm bones. So, *T. rex* must have been able to move its arms. What did *T. rex* use its arms to do? Scientists who study dinosaurs still do not know for sure.

Another question is whether *T. rex* had scaly skin. The fossils of *T. rex* show the bones, but not the skin. Newly discovered fossils show that some dinosaurs had feathers. Scientists think it is possible that *T. rex* was also covered in fuzzy feathers, at least when it was young. Even if that were so, you probably would not want to snuggle with a baby *T. rex*!

Fossils show *T. rex* had small arms. Scientists are still not sure how *T. rex* used its arms.

What Do Fossils Show About Environments of Long Ago?

Scientists can learn a lot about environments by studying the organisms that live there. They can also learn about the environments of long ago by studying fossils of organisms that once lived there. For instance, mammoth fossils teach scientists about the environments that mammoths once lived in.

NGSS **3-LS4-1.** Analyze and interpret data from fossils to provide evidence of the organisms and the environments in which they lived long ago.

LS4.A. • Some kinds of plants and animals that once lived on Earth are no longer found anywhere. • Fossils provide evidence about the types of organisms that lived long ago and also about the nature of their environments.

Scale, Proportion, and Quantity Observable phenomena exist from very short to very long time periods.

Analyzing and Interpreting Data

1. Environments Change over Millions of Years

Scientists have found ocean fossils on the tops of mountains. How did those fossils get there?

You have learned that environments can change. They can change a lot over a long period of time. Rocks made of fossil coral at the top of a mountain were once under the ocean. Fish, corals, and other animals lived in this ocean. But over millions of years, the environment changed. The land was slowly lifted up by motions like earthquakes. The water flowed away and the ocean dried up. Today, the area is a mountaintop!

Fossils of palm tree stumps have been found in Antarctica. Today, Antarctica is very cold and snowy. But palm trees live in warm places. They could not live in Antarctica today. They grew in Antarctica when it was warmer a long time ago.

Environments can change over long periods of time. That is why coral fossils like this one are sometimes found on mountaintops.

Nature of Science

2. Studying Old Environments

Suppose you saw an animal with thick fur in a zoo. What environment might that animal be from?

Adaptations and Environments

Each kind of organism is adapted to its own environment. You can learn a lot about a place by looking at the organisms that live there. Many animals are adapted to living in a cold place. They often have thick fur that keeps them warm.

Fish are adapted to living in water. They have *gills* and *fins*. Fish use their gills to breathe underwater. Fins help them swim. You can be sure that an animal with gills and fins lives in water.

Gills and fins are adaptations that help an animal live in water. Finding a fossil with gills and fins shows that an area used to be under water.

Scientists learn about past environments by looking at fossils. Fossils hold clues. Their adaptations show that an organism lived in a certain type of place. We can compare a fossil's adaptations to the adaptations of creatures that are alive today and learn about its environment.

Gills

Fins

This model of an extinct woolly mammoth shows its thick fur. Scientists can infer that mammoths lived in cold environments because of fossil fur and other evidence.

An Organism's Adaptations and Its Environment Are Linked

Organisms have been on Earth for more than 3 billion years. They, as well as the places where they have lived, have changed many times. Fossils give clues about the changes.

If you found a fossil of an extinct animal that had gills and fins, you could *infer* that place was once under water. To **infer** means to use evidence to draw a conclusion.

Scientists infer that the link between an organism's adaptations and where it lives stays the same. Suppose you find a fossil of an extinct animal with thick fur that lived 2 million years ago. You know that animals alive today with thick fur live in cold places. You can infer or conclude that the extinct animal lived in a cold place. If the place had been very warm, the animal would not have needed the warm fur coat.

These are models of Spinosaurus dinosaurs. They lived in wetlands where they ate many fish.

3. Studying Dinosaurs' Environments

Millions of years ago, dinosaurs lived all over Earth. They lived only on land, but there were many land environments.

Wet Environments

Wet areas were home to many kinds of dinosaurs. Swamps, rivers, and *wetlands* were common. **Wetlands** are low, soggy areas where land and water meet.

Fossils show that river banks and seashores were covered with ferns and trees. Plant-eating dinosaurs lived there at the same time as these plants. Their fossils show that they had strong, flat teeth like animals that eat plants today. So these teeth were adapted for chewing plants. Dinosaurs that ate fish lived in swamps. Their fossils look like modern crocodiles with long snouts. When scientists find fossils like these, they infer things about the environment that the dinosaurs lived in.

Dry Environments

Plains and deserts were drier places. Plains were covered with small plants. Large numbers of fossil bones and teeth from plant-eating dinosaurs have been found in places that used to be plains. They show that herds of these dinosaurs lived together. They ate the plants. Large numbers of fossil footprints also show that these animals lived in groups. Meat eaters ate the plant eaters.

Fewer plants grew in deserts. So, many desert dinosaurs were meat eaters. A fossil found in a desert in China shows a meat-eating dinosaur attacking a plant eater.

Deserts and plains are wide open places. They were good homes for dinosaurs with long legs that ran after prey. Many fossils found in these areas have long, strong leg bones.

These pieces of fossilized bone are from a dinosaur that lived in the desert. Scientists learn about the environments dinosaurs lived in when they study fossils.

This is an artist's version of what a large space rock hitting Earth could look like. Many scientists think a rock that hit Earth about 65 million years ago is what killed the large dinosaurs.

4. Dinosaur Extinction

Dinosaurs all over the world died at about the same time. What could have happened to them?

Often, extinctions are caused by several changes. From fossils, scientists have inferred that dinosaurs lived for almost 200 million years. Then all of the large dinosaurs suddenly went extinct about 65 million years ago. A huge rock from space also crashed into Earth about 65 million years ago. Many scientists have inferred that this is what killed the dinosaurs. The crash threw huge clouds of dust into the air and cooled the whole planet. Without light, plants would have died. Then dinosaurs would have died, too.

Other scientists found evidence that a huge volcano erupted. Maybe it killed most of the dinosaurs. Whatever happened, the large dinosaurs were not adapted to their changed environment. They could no longer survive. Scientists are still trying to understand what happened.

What Do Fossils Show About Environments of Long Ago?

1. Environments Change over Millions of Years
Environments can change a lot over a very long period of time. Fossils of plants and animals can show scientists what an area used to be like. Coral fossils found on a mountaintop shows that the land was once under an ocean. Palm tree fossils show that an area was once warm.

2. Studying Old Environments   Scientists can learn what environments are like today by studying the organisms that live there. Creatures that look a certain way only live in certain kinds of places. Fossils of organisms can show what environments were like long ago.

3. Studying Dinosaurs' Environments   Dinosaurs lived in many places on Earth. By studying their fossils, scientists have learned that some dinosaurs lived in wet environments, like wetlands. Other dinosaurs lived in dry environments, like deserts.

4. Dinosaur Extinction   The large dinosaurs went extinct about 66 million years ago. That is also when a large rock from space crashed into Earth, which may have killed them. The mystery is still being solved, but more than one thing probably happened. When their environment changed, the organisms that could not adapt, died.

Dino Droppings

Scientists can learn about the environments of the dinosaurs by studying fossilized bones. One other type of fossil can tell scientists exactly what dinosaurs ate.

If you had to choose between meeting a real live *Tyrannosaurus rex* and a *Triceratops horridus*, which would you choose? Both dinosaurs were about the size of a bus. Both had strong jaws and lots of sharp teeth. Most people would probably choose to stay away from *T. rex*. This is because they know that *T. rex* ate other animals. But how do people know for sure? Could *T. Rex* have spent its days grazing on grass?

One clue to the diet of the *T. rex* is its large, knife-like teeth. They are perfect for tearing into meat. Scientists have found *T. rex* bite marks in the fossils of other dinosaurs. They even found a fossil of *T. Rex* teeth that broke off in the bones of victims. But teeth are not the only clues that dinosaurs left lying around. They also left prehistoric droppings!

You can learn about *Tyrannosaurus rex* and *Triceratops horridus* by studying their fossils.

More Than Just Stones

Animal droppings are also called scat. You can learn a lot about an animal—even a dinosaur—from its scat.

Looking for dinosaur scat might sound like an unpleasant job. But remember, the dinosaur scat is not fresh. It is a trace fossil now. Fossilized scat are not at all stinky. They look like ordinary rocks.

In fact, until the 1800s, most people just thought that was all they were. Then a British girl named Mary Anning noticed a pattern. She found fossil bones of huge animals by the seashore. She noticed certain kinds of rocks were often found with the fossil bones. When she broke open the mysterious rocks, she found pieces of fish bones. The rocks were actually fossilized scat. The scat provided evidence of the giant creature's dinner.

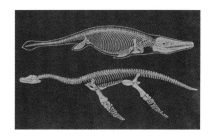

Mary Anning discovered fossil skeletons of these huge ancient animals. She also found fossilized scat near the fossil bones.

Once animal scat becomes a trace fossil, it can look like a rock.

The fossil bone inside this fossilized scat shows that the animal that made it ate other animals.

Animal or Vegetable?

Cracking open dinosaur scat can be like opening a present. The surprise inside is discovering what kind of meal the dinosaur ate.

Inside the scat are pieces of food waste. This was food that passed through the dinosaur. The food waste may have been bones, like the fossil fish bones Mary Anning found. The waste may also have been fur, fish scales, or shells. Fossil waste becomes clues showing the kinds of animals the dinosaur ate. Plant-eating dinosaurs left clues in their scat, too. Their scat may hold fossils of seeds or other plant parts.

A dinosaur's scat also gives clues about its environment. It shows that the dinosaur and its meal lived in the same place. An animal that ate fish must have lived in or near water. One that ate parts of trees probably did not live in the sea. Of course, you can only infer this if you can match the dinosaur to its scat.

Scattered Clues

How do you know which animal left the scat? It was easy for Mary Anning because the fossilized scat she found was right next to the fossils of the animals that made it. But fossil scat is almost never found with a dinosaur fossil. Instead, scientists look for other clues that show what animal passed the scat.

Shape is one clue. The scat of ancient sharks is spiral shaped. Finding a piece of fossilized shark scat in an area can show that a sea once covered the place.

Size is another clue. Large dinosaurs likely left large droppings. One piece of scat found by a scientist was more than 30 cm (1 ft) long! It was filled with crushed bones. It was not hard to conclude what could leave scat like that. Only a *T. rex* could leave such a dropping!

The Maiasaura was a large dinosaur that ate plants. Its scat has wood in it. This shows the dinosaur lived in a land environment with trees.

Forces and Motion

On a summer day, you and your family go to the fair. There, you go on a ride that spins you around! When the ride starts, you move slowly. Your feet are now off the ground. It starts to spin faster, and you feel yourself moving up higher. In this unit, you will learn how pushes and pulls change how objects move.

Unit Contents

Unit 2 Overview

Graphic Organizer: This unit is structured to first define **forces**, then teach how forces are used to **make predictions**, and finally explore **noncontact forces**.

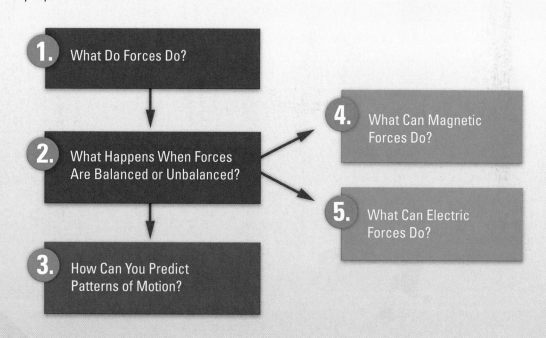

1. What Do Forces Do?

2. What Happens When Forces Are Balanced or Unbalanced?

3. How Can You Predict Patterns of Motion?

4. What Can Magnetic Forces Do?

5. What Can Electric Forces Do?

NGSS Next Generation Science Standards

Performance Expectations

3-PS2-1. Plan and conduct an investigation to provide evidence of the effects of balanced and unbalanced forces on the motion of an object.

3-PS2-2. Make observations and/or measurements of an object's motion to provide evidence that a pattern can be used to predict future motion.

3-PS2-3. Ask questions to determine cause and effect relationships of electric or magnetic interactions between two objects not in contact with each other.

3-PS2-4. Define a simple design problem that can be solved by applying scientific ideas about magnets.

Disciplinary Core Ideas

PS2.A: Forces and Motion

- Each force acts on one particular object and has both strength and a direction. An object at rest typically has multiple forces acting on it, but they add to give zero net force on the object. Forces that do not sum to zero can cause changes in the object's speed or direction of motion.

- The patterns of an object's motion in various situations can be observed and measured; when that past motion exhibits a regular pattern, future motion can be predicted from it.

PS2.B: Types of Interactions

- Objects in contact exert forces on each other.

- Electric and magnetic forces between a pair of objects do not require that the objects be in contact. The sizes of the forces in each situation depend on the properties of the objects and their distances apart and, for forces between two magnets, on their orientation relative to each other.

Crosscutting Concepts

Patterns

- Patterns of change can be used to make predictions.

Cause and Effect

- Cause and effect relationships are routinely identified.

- Cause and effect relationships are routinely identified, tested, and used to explain change.

 Asking Questions and Defining Problems

 Planning and Carrying Out Investigations

Have you ever wondered...

If you push or pull on an object, you can observe how it moves. This unit will help you answer these questions and many others you may ask.

Why do some things stick to magnets?

Why does a ball move when I kick it?

What makes a swing move back and forth?

What Do Forces Do?

Science Vocabulary

force

motion

position

Think of a time when you saw an object move. As it moved, its position changed. A moving object has speed and direction. But pushing or pulling the object can cause its speed and direction to change. You will learn what can affect the speed and direction of objects.

NGSS | **3-PS2-1.** Plan and conduct an investigation to provide evidence of the effects of balanced and unbalanced forces on the motion of an object.

PS2.A. Each force acts on one particular object and has both strength and a direction. An object at rest typically has multiple forces acting on it, but they add to give zero net force on the object. Forces that do not sum to zero can cause changes in the object's speed or direction of motion.
PS2.B. Objects in contact exert forces on each other.

Cause and Effect Cause and effect relationships are routinely identified.

Planning and Carrying Out Investigations

1. Motion Is a Change in Position

You are watching a race in which the runners start on one part of the track. But during the race, they move to another part. They are in *motion*.

Motion is a change in the *position* of an object. **Position** is an object's location compared to its surroundings. When an object is in motion, you can see it change position. For example, a runner begins a race behind the start line, but after the race starts, she appears in front of the line. Her position compared to the start line has changed. This is because she is in motion.

Motion is described by its direction and speed. *Direction* is which way an object moves. These runners are running forward on the track. They move in the same direction. *Speed* is how fast an object moves. One runner runs ahead of the others. The runners move at different speeds.

When something is in motion, it changes position. These runners are in motion, so as they move, their positions change compared to the start line.

2. Forces Are Pushes and Pulls

You can observe motion in a baseball game. The pitcher throws the ball toward home plate. Then the batter hits the ball, and it moves away from home plate quickly. After the batter hits the ball, the ball's direction and speed change.

When the batter hits the ball, he puts a *force* on the ball. A **force** is a push or pull. The batter pulls the bat backward then pushes it forward. When the bat hits the ball, it pushes the ball.

You put forces on objects all the time. Your fingers push on keys when you type on a computer's keyboard, and they pull on a page in a book when you turn it. Your feet push off the ground when you walk.

Nonliving objects also can put forces on objects. A bulldozer pushes dirt, a train engine pulls train cars, and wind pushes leaves off trees.

When you type on a computer keyboard, turn a page, or walk, you put forces on objects. When you put a force on an object, you either push or pull it.

When two people arm wrestle, their hands put forces on each other. If you arm wrestle with a friend, your hand pushes your friend's hand. Your friend's hand also pushes your hand. There are two forces at work when your hands push against each other. Even if your hands just touch, there are two forces at work. There are small forces pushing between your hands.

Forces change the speed and direction of an object's motion. Suppose you kick a soccer ball to your friend. When you kick the ball, you put a force on it, and the force causes the ball to move quickly away from you. When your friend kicks the ball back, she puts another force on it. That force changes the ball's motion so that it moves at a different speed and in another direction.

When you kick a soccer ball, you put a force on it. That force changes the speed and direction of the ball's motion.

Forces have strength and direction. A forklift pushes a rock upward with a strong force, while a person pushes the doorbell forward with a weak force.

3. Forces Have Strength and Direction

When you hit a baseball, you put a force on it. You can hit the ball hard or just tap it. You can hit the ball toward left field or right field. The force put on the ball affects the ball's motion.

Forces have strength and direction. *Strength* is how hard a force pushes or pulls. A forklift is a machine that lifts heavy objects. It pushes with a strong force to move big rocks. A person pushes with a weak force to ring a doorbell. *Direction* is which way a force pushes or pulls. The forklift's force pushes the heavy rock upward. The person's force pushes the doorbell forward.

An object can put force that is strong at one time and weak at another time on another object. For example, you lift a heavy book with a strong force, but you lift a pencil with a weak force.

Two forces can have the same strength but different directions. Volleyball players put forces on a ball when they hit it. Suppose one player hits the ball backward. Then another player uses the same amount of strength to hit the ball forward. The two forces have the same strength, but they have different directions.

Two forces can also have the same direction but different strengths. Suppose both volleyball players hit the ball forward. One player hits it hard, but the other player hits it softly. The forces push in the same direction, but their strengths are different. They make the ball move at different speeds.

A force has strength and direction. A force's strength and direction can affect which way an object moves and how fast it moves.

These volleyball players can hit the ball in different directions using the same strength.

4. Forces Change Motion

You know a force has strength and direction. How can a force change an object's motion?

Forces can affect a hockey puck's motion. A hockey player moves a puck forward, and he pushes it just enough to keep the puck in front of him. Then he hits the puck with a stronger force to a teammate on his left. The force changes the puck's speed, so it goes faster. It also changes the puck's direction from forward to leftward.

The teammate uses a force to block the puck with his stick. That force briefly slows the puck's speed and stops it moving leftward. Quickly, he hits the puck toward the goal. That force increases the puck's speed again and changes its direction to a forward motion.

So, a force changes the motion of an object. It can speed up, slow down, or turn an object.

When this hockey player hits the puck, he changes its direction and speed. A single force can change the direction and speed of an object.

What Do Forces Do?

1. Motion Is a Change in Position   An object's position is its location compared to its surroundings. If the object changes its position, it is in motion. The object's motion has both direction and speed.

2. Forces Are Pushes and Pulls   When you put a force on an object, you are either pushing or pulling the object. When two objects touch, they are putting forces on each other. Forces can change the speed and direction of an object's motion.

3. Forces Have Strength and Direction   Strength is how hard a force pushes or pulls. Direction is which way a force pushes or pulls. Two forces can have the same direction but different strengths. They can also have the same strengths but different directions.

4. Forces Change Motion   Forces have both strength and direction, and they can change the motion of objects. How the object's motion changes depends on the force's strength and direction. A force can speed up, slow down, or turn an object.

Fair Forces

When you play games at the fair, you use forces to move balls, beanbags, and rings. But to *win* a game, you have to apply a force that has just the right strength and direction.

"Step right up! Try your luck, and win a prize!" You are at the fair, ready for fun! While heading for the roller coaster, someone calls out to you from a game booth. The game looks very easy. Why not give it a try?

Carnival games at fairs and amusement parks look very easy. All you have to do is knock over a tower of tin cans or throw a ball in a bucket. But carnival games are not always as easy as they appear. You can spend hours playing a game and still not win a single prize. But it is possible to win if you put the right forces to work.

In this game, all you have to do is knock over tin cans with a ball. Even though it looks easy, you have to use the right amount of force to win!

In One Ball, you have to knock over three bottles with one ball. To win, aim the ball so that it hits the bases of the bottom two bottles.

One Ball

Your first stop is a game called One Ball. In this game, you must knock over three bottles with just one toss of a ball. You aim for the spot where the bottles meet and throw. Direct hit! But only the top bottle goes flying. The other two bottles wobble but stay standing. Why does this happen?

You might think that you should hit all three bottles with the ball. But the bottles are heavier on the bottom than they are on the top. The heavy bottoms make the bottles hard to topple. So, what should you do?

To topple the tower, you have to apply a force to the place where the two bottom bottles touch the platform. You also have to throw the ball so that it hits the bottles with a very strong force. If the force is strong enough, they will fall. The top bottle will then fall, too.

To win at Flukey Ball, you need to toss the ball in certain way. The ball needs to follow a path that is shaped like an arc.

Flukey Ball

The next game you try is called Flukey Ball. In this game, you have to toss a ball so that it hits a board and then lands in a basket. It looks just like basketball. So, it should be easy, right?

The board in Flukey Ball is not like one in basketball. Instead, it is tilted upward. So, when the ball hits the board, the force pushes the ball up and away from the basket.

The secret to winning the game is to toss the ball upward so that the ball travels in an arc. If you throw the ball correctly, it will just brush the bottom of the board on the way down. The small force causes the ball to land in the basket. But you have to toss the ball gently. If the ball hits the board too hard, the force will be too strong. The ball will then bounce away.

Squirt Blaster Races

The last game you try at the fair is called Squirt Blaster Race. In this game, you aim a stream of water from a blaster at a target. When you hit the target, a toy horse moves along a track. The horse that reaches the end first wins!

Once again, forces are key. But this time, a blaster applies the force. Before you play, watch other people play. Observe the water coming out of the blasters. Find the blaster that pushes water out with the strongest force. A blaster that shoots with a strong force throws the water farther. That makes hitting the target easier.

As you can see, games at fairs can be tricky. But knowing about forces can help you win. When you see people who have won big prizes at the fair, they might not be athletes. Instead, they might be scientists who know about forces!

If you want to win at Squirt Blaster Race, observe other players. Then find the blaster that has the strongest stream.

What Happens When Forces Are Balanced or Unbalanced?

Science Vocabulary

balanced forces

gravity

unbalanced forces

As these students arm wrestle, they push with equal strength. Whose hand will move? A force can change an object's motion. But sometimes if you push or pull an object, its motion will not change. You will learn how balanced and unbalanced forces acting on an object affect its motion.

NGSS

3-PS2-1. Plan and conduct an investigation to provide evidence of the effects of balanced and unbalanced forces on the motion of an object.

PS2.A. Each force acts on one particular object and has both strength and a direction. An object at rest typically has multiple forces acting on it, but they add to give zero net force on the object. Forces that do not sum to zero can cause changes in the object's speed or direction of motion.

Cause and Effect Cause and effect relationships are routinely identified.

Planning and Carrying Out Investigations

1. Adding Forces

Did you ever try to push a heavy object by yourself? Some objects are so heavy that you cannot move them easily. The force you put on the object is not strong enough to move it. So, you might try to push the object with a friend.

When more than one force pushes in the same direction, you can add the forces together and get a stronger force. This is why you might need a friend to help move an object that you cannot move alone.

Suppose someone wants to lift and move a sofa. He pulls the sofa upward. It only moves a little. But if he and a friend pull the sofa upward together, the sofa moves more. Their forces add together when they push in the same direction. The combined force is strong enough to lift and move the sofa.

These people are pulling a sofa upward together. When more than one force pulls or pushes on an object in the same direction, the forces add together.

During this game of tug-of-war, two teams pull on the rope with equal strength in opposite directions. Because balanced forces act on the rope, the rope's motion does not change.

2. Forces in Balance

Have you ever played tug-of-war? In this game, two teams pull a rope in opposite directions. Each team tries to pull the other team to their side. What kind of forces will not change the rope's motion?

If two teams pull with the same strength, the forces are balanced. **Balanced forces** are forces that together do not cause a change in motion. For example, two forces that push or pull in opposite directions with equal strength are balanced forces.

Two teams are about to begin a game of tug-of-war. The teams start pulling on the rope, but the rope does not move. This is because balanced forces are acting on the rope. The two teams are pulling on the rope in opposite directions with equal strength.

Suppose that a box sits on a table. Then two people start pushing it in opposite directions. The forces pushing on the box are equal in strength. The box does not move, which means the forces acting on the box are balanced.

Forces act on objects even when they are still. An apple rests on a hand. What forces are acting on the apple? One force called *gravity* is pulling the apple down. **Gravity** is a force that pulls down. But gravity does not pull the apple all the way to the ground. This is because another force is pushing the apple in the opposite direction. The hand is pushing up the apple.

The apple is still, so its motion does not change. This means that balanced forces are acting on it. Gravity is pulling down the apple and the hand is pushing up the apple with equal strength.

Gravity pulls down the apple with the same strength that that the hand pushes up the apple. The apple's motion does not change because balanced forces are acting on it.

Hand pushes up

Gravity pulls down

One team is pulling with a more strength than the other team, so there are unbalanced forces. Unbalanced forces acting on the rope cause the rope's motion to change.

3. Forces Not in Balance

You know that an object's motion does not change when balanced forces act on it. When do forces cause an object's motion to change?

During a game of tug-of-war, one team pulls the rope with more strength than the other does. If the teams pull with unequal strength, the forces are unbalanced. **Unbalanced forces** are forces that together cause a change in motion. Two forces that push or pull in opposite directions with unequal strength are unbalanced forces.

How can unbalanced forces change a rope's motion? During a game of tug-of-war, two teams are pulling with equal strength. Then one team starts pulling on the rope with more strength. The rope starts moving faster and faster toward the team pulling harder. The rope's motion changed because unbalanced forces were acting on it.

What happens as you throw a ball upward? The force of your throw pushes the ball upward. At the same time, gravity pulls it downward. The force of your throw is stronger than gravity. The forces are unbalanced, so the ball's motion changes. The ball starts moving upward.

What happens after you throw the ball? After you let go of it, the ball keeps moving upward. But after it leaves your hand, the only force acting on the ball is gravity. Gravity pulls down on the upward moving ball. The unbalanced forces change the ball's motion. First, its speed changes. The ball starts to move upward slower. Soon, the ball stops for an instant. Then, it changes direction. It begins to move downward as gravity keeps pulling on it. It falls faster and faster until it hits the ground.

These students' hands pushed up on the balls with more force than gravity pulled down on them. The unbalanced forces caused the balls to start moving upward.

4. Measuring Forces

How much force is needed to zip up a backpack? To find the answer, you need to be able to measure the strength of forces.

Scientists use different methods and tools to measure force. One tool they use is a *spring scale*. A scientist wants to know how much force it takes to hold an object up in the air. He attaches the tool to the object. When he holds it up, the spring inside the tool stretches. The marked number on the scale shows how much force it took to hold the object up in the air.

A *dynamometer* is another tool that scientists use to measure force. A scientist wants to measure how much force medical patients can squeeze with. She asks patients to put their hands around the tool and squeeze. The marked number on the scale shows how much force is put on it.

A spring scale (left) is a tool that measures how much force is needed to hold an object in the air. A dynamometer (right) is a tool that measures how much force a person squeezes with.

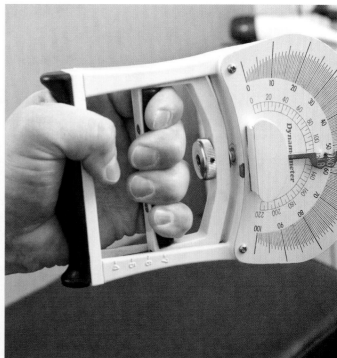

What Happens When Forces Are Balanced or Unbalanced?

1. Adding Forces A force may push on an object, but the object may not move. But when more than one force pushes on the object in the same direction, the forces add together, and you get a stronger force.

2. Forces in Balance Balanced forces are forces that together do not cause a change in motion. When two forces of the same strength push or pull in opposite directions, the forces are balanced forces. When balanced forces act on an object, the object's motion does not change.

3. Forces Not in Balance Unbalanced forces are forces that together cause a change in motion. When two forces pushing or pulling in opposite directions are not the same strength, the forces are unbalanced forces. When unbalanced forces act on an object, the object's motion changes.

4. Measuring Forces Scientists use different tools to measure force. A spring scale and a dynamometer are two tools that scientists use to measure the strength of forces.

"5, 4, 3, 2, 1—Lift Off!"

Getting a huge and heavy spacecraft into space is not easy. How does a spacecraft overcome the force of gravity to leave Earth?

It's May 31, 2008. Space shuttle *Discovery* is waiting on the launch pad. Inside, astronaut Karen Nyberg is ready for her first trip into space. She hears the voice of Mission Control. "We go for main engine start! 7, 6, 5, 4, 3, 2, 1—booster ignition and LIFT OFF!"

Nyberg feels the shuttle shake as fuel in rocket engines burn. The explosion sends gases spewing out from the bottom of the rockets. The gases push upward with a huge force. This upward force grows until it is larger than the force of gravity pulling the rockets down. The forces are now unbalanced. The upward force overcomes gravity's downward force, so the shuttle's rockets move away from the ground. Nyberg can feel the shuttle moving faster and faster as it heads for space.

A rocket pushes upward with a force that is greater than gravity, so it moves upward toward space.

In space, Nyberg and the other astronauts appear weightless. They float inside of the shuttle. It seems like there is no gravity.

Even though objects in a space shuttle seem weightless, there is actually gravity in space. The shuttle moves very fast around Earth. Gravity pulls the shuttle toward Earth, keeping it in orbit. The objects inside of the shuttle are also falling toward Earth because of gravity. But they are falling at the same speed and in the same direction as the space shuttle. The shuttle and objects inside of it move at the same speed, so the objects float in the air.

Nyberg shows how life in space is both fun and challenging because objects seem weightless. She has taken photos of objects floating. She has even made a video of washing her long hair as it floats away from her head. It's not easy to do!

In space, objects appear weightless even though there is gravity. This photo shows how Nyberg's hair floats in the space shuttle.

How Can You Predict Patterns of Motion?

Science Vocabulary

predict

How do you think this swing will move next? You will learn about the patterns objects move in. If you study these patterns, you can learn how forces change the motion of an object. Studying patterns of motion can also tell you how an object might move in the future.

 NGSS   **3-PS2-2.** Make observations and/or measurements of an object's motion to provide evidence that a pattern can be used to predict future motion.   **PS2.A.** The patterns of an object's motion in various situations can be observed and measured; when that past motion exhibits a regular pattern, future motion can be predicted from it.   **Patterns** Patterns of change can be used to make predictions.    **Planning and Carrying Out Investigations**

Nature of Science

1. Observing Patterns of Motion

When you push a friend on a swing, the swing goes back and forth many times. It moves in the same pattern each time.

Scientists look for patterns when they observe objects in motion. They classify motion by its patterns. One pattern is back-and-forth motion. A second pattern is motion in a line. A third pattern is motion in a circle.

You can observe motion and find a pattern. When a swing moves, you see a pattern of back-and-forth motion. When a ball rolls, you observe a pattern of motion in a line. When a pinwheel spins around, you see a pattern of motion in a circle. Patterns of motion repeat, so you can observe objects move in the same pattern over and over again.

Scientists classify motion by its patterns. What pattern of motion do you think the bowling ball moves in? What about the pinwheel?

2. Explaining Patterns of Motion

You know that objects can move back and forth, in a line, or in a circle. How do you think each pattern of motion works?

How does back-and-forth motion work? You know that gravity is a force that pulls down. So, when a swing is pushed, it moves upward at first. But as it goes up, gravity keeps pulling down on it. Unbalanced forces cause the swing's motion to change. The swing slows down to a stop. Then it changes direction and moves down.

As it moves down, the swing also moves back. The swing hangs from chains on a pole, so as it moves downward, the chains also pull back on it. The force pulls the swing with enough strength that it moves backward and then up in the air. Then gravity pulls the swing down again. The back-and-forth pattern continues.

Gravity pulls down on the swing, and the chains pull the swing to the pole it hangs from. These forces keep the swing moving back and forth after it is pushed.

Back-and-Forth Motion

Chain pulls backward

Gravity pulls down

Motion in a Circle

Rope pulls toward pole

When someone hit this tetherball, it moved away from the pole, but the rope pulls the ball back toward the center of the pole. The unbalanced forces cause the ball to move in a circle around the pole.

How does motion in a line work? Kick a soccer ball. Unbalanced forces cause it to move away from your foot. The ball is not attached to another object, so it is not pulled back. It moves forward in a line until another force acts on it. If someone else kicks the ball, the ball's speed and direction changes, but it still moves in a line.

How does motion in a circle work? The end of a tetherball rope is connected to the top of a pole. So, as the ball moves, the pole pulls the rope and ball toward its center. This keeps the forces unbalanced, so the ball keeps moving in a circle around the pole. If you cut the rope so the pole does not pull on the ball, the ball's pattern of motion changes. It moves away from the pole in a line instead of around the pole in a circle.

If you know that the jump rope moves in a circle when you spin it, you can predict that it will keep moving in a circle if you keep spinning it. But if a new force is added, then the pattern will change.

3. Predicting Patterns of Motion

When you push a swing, it moves back and forth. How will it move if you push it again?

You can *predict* that the swing will move back and forth. To **predict** means to use what you know to tell what might happen in the future. If the force is the same, the object will move the same way.

If a new force is added, the pattern changes. You and a friend spin a jump rope, so it moves in a circle. Then your friend yanks the rope away, so you let go of it. The rope stops moving in a circle. The rope's end moves away from you in a line.

You can find patterns between objects to predict motion. A ball is not attached to anything, so if you push it, it is not pulled back. It moves in a line. What will happen if you push a toy car? A toy car is also not attached to anything, so you can predict that it will move in a line if you push it.

How Can You Predict Patterns of Motion?

1. Observing Patterns of Motion   When scientists observe objects in motion, they look for patterns. They use patterns to classify motion. Patterns of motion include back-and-forth motion, motion in a line, and motion in a circle. You can observe motion and find patterns, too.

2. Explaining Patterns of Motion   You can explain how each pattern of motion works. You know that unbalanced forces cause a change in motion. If you observe what forces are put on an object, you can explain why a swing moves back and forth, a ball moves in a straight line, and a tetherball moves in a circle.

3. Predicting Patterns of Motion   You can use what you know about forces and motion to predict how an object will move. But if a new force is introduced, the object's pattern of motion will change. You can also find patterns between objects to predict motion.

'Round and 'Round They Go

Like the swings on a carnival ride, a satellite that orbits Earth spins around and around in a circular motion.

The motion of a swing ride starts slowly. As it picks up speed, the swings fly outward. They feel like they will fly away! But its ropes apply an unbalanced force toward the center of the ride that keeps the swing moving in a circle.

Like the swing, a satellite also moves in a circular motion. But no rope pulls the satellite around Earth. Instead, gravity is the unbalanced force that keeps satellites moving in a circle.

Hundreds of satellites orbit Earth. Some of those satellites are *geostationary*. Geostationary satellites stay above one spot on Earth at all times. Picture a geostationary satellite above your home. As Earth turns, the satellite would move with it. So, the satellite would always be above your home.

This was the first geostationary satellite to be put into orbit. A geostationary satellite stays above one spot on Earth at all times.

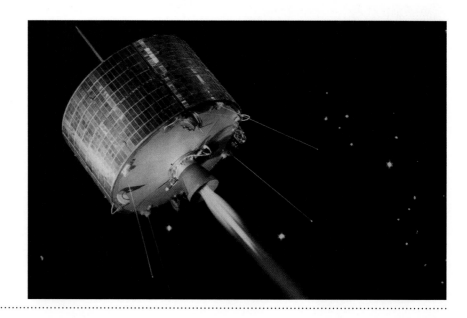

Using Satellites

Many geostationary satellites orbit Earth. But what are these satellites used for?

Satellite TV is one way people use geostationary satellites. Satellite TV starts when a station on Earth sends a signal to a satellite in space. The satellite then sends the signal back to an area on Earth. The small dishes that you see on homes pick up signals from the satellite.

Geostationary satellites are also used to gather data about weather. Weather satellites take photos of Earth. Some of these photos show clouds. Other photos show temperature. Some even show how much water is in the air. Scientists then use these images to predict the weather.

These TV satellite dishes recieve signals from a geostationary satellite.

Geostationary satellites are used to capture images of Earth, like this one. These images help scientists predict the weather.

Inside of this white, cone-shaped covering is a geostationary satellite. Engineers designed the satellite to collect data about weather.

Designing Satellites

Geostationary satellites are used for many things. So, not all satellites are the same. Each one is specially designed by engineers.

Engineers have to consider many things when designing a satellite. They have to consider a satellite's size and shape. They also have to think about what tools the satellite will use. For example, a satellite that collects data about weather might use cameras or sensors.

Satellite engineers also have to think about force and motion. You learned that gravity pulls a satellite toward Earth. In order for a satellite to get into orbit around Earth, it has to move at a very quick speed. If the satellite is not moving fast enough, it will fall back to Earth. So, engineers make sure that a satellite moves at the right speed when they launch it.

A Bumpy Ride

Engineers also think about force and motion to help satellites stay in orbit. They make sure that the speed of a satellite and the gravity that pulls on it are just right. If the satellite slows down too much, it will fall back to Earth. If it speeds up too much, it will fly away into space.

In space, a satellite can get bumped by other objects. These objects include old satellites and parts of a rocket. The force of these objects can change a satellite's speed. So, a satellite sometimes needs to correct its orbit. Engineers put rockets on satellites. The rockets help correct a satellite's orbit when it gets bumped by other objects.

These white dots are objects flying through space. Many of them are satellites. Sometimes these objects collide with each other.

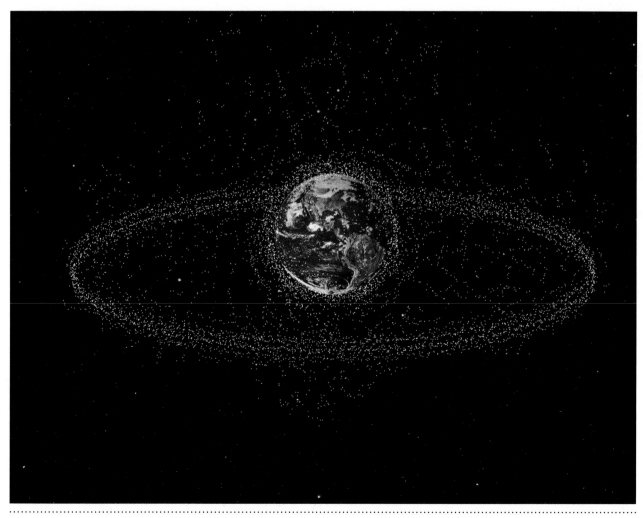

What Can Magnetic Forces Do?

Science Vocabulary

electromagnet

magnetic force

permanent magnet

This magnet is pulling up metal in a scrap yard. How can the magnet change the metal's motion? You will learn that a magnet can affect an object's motion without touching it because of magnetic forces. Engineers use what they know about magnets to solve problems.

NGSS

3-PS2-3. Ask questions to determine cause and effect relationships of electric or magnetic interactions between two objects not in contact with each other.
3-PS2-4. Define a simple design problem that can be solved by applying scientific ideas about magnets.

PS2.B. Electric and magnetic forces between a pair of objects do not require that the objects be in contact. The sizes of the forces in each situation depend on the properties of the objects and their distances apart and, for forces between two magnets, on their orientation relative to each other.

Cause and Effect Cause and effect relationships are routinely identified, tested, and used to explain change.

Asking Questions and Defining Problems

1. Magnetic Forces

Do you hang pictures on the refrigerator door at home? You can use magnets to hold them up.

Magnets stick to refrigerators because of *magnetic forces*. **Magnetic force** is a push or pull between two or more magnets or between a magnet and certain types of metal. Objects do not need to touch for magnetic forces to work. Put a magnet close to, but not touching, another magnet. They will either push or pull each other.

How can you predict how magnets will affect each other? Every magnet has a *north pole* and a *south pole*. *Unlike* poles attract. A north pole and south pole are unlike. So, when these poles face each other, they pull toward each other.

Poles that are the same, or *like* poles, repel. Two north poles are like poles. They push away from each other. Two south poles are also like poles. They repel, too.

These magnets repel each other. Are unlike or like poles facing each other?

On these magnets, *N* marks the north poles, and *S* marks the south poles. Unlike poles attract each other, and like poles repel.

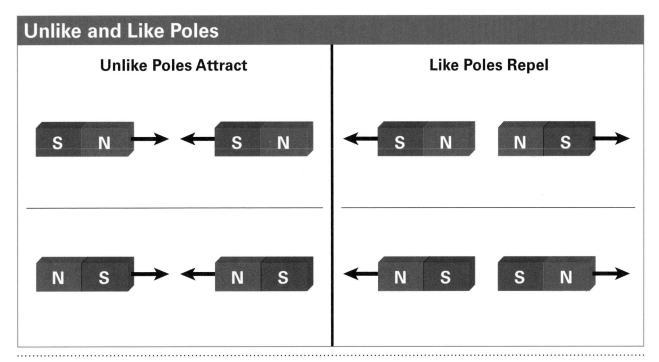

Unlike and Like Poles

Unlike Poles Attract	Like Poles Repel

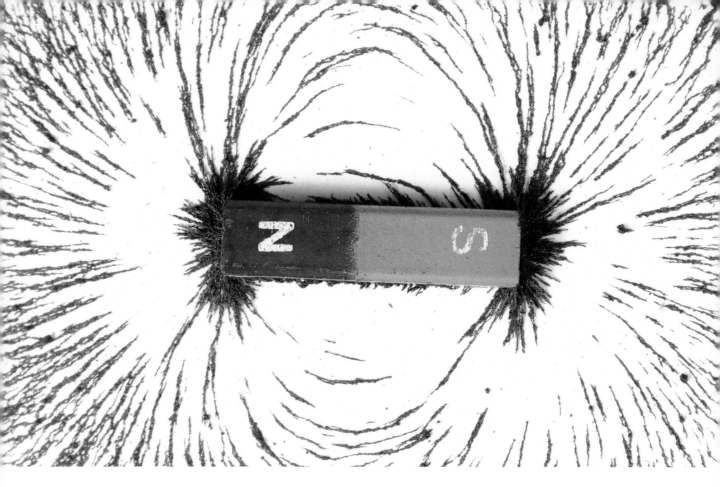

Most of the iron filings are attracted to the ends of this magnet. Magnetic forces are strongest near the poles of a magnet.

2. Stronger and Weaker Magnetic Forces

A magnet pulls iron filings toward it. But it can only pull the iron if it is close enough. Where and when are magnetic forces strongest?

Magnetic forces are strongest near the poles of a magnet. Put a bar magnet near iron filings. If you do this, most of the iron will move toward the ends, or the poles, of the magnet.

Hold two magnets close together. Put the north pole of one near the south pole of the other. You can feel the magnetic force pulling them together. Magnetic forces are strong when objects are very close.

Now hold the magnets farther apart. The pull feels weaker if you hold them away from each other. This is because magnetic forces are weaker between objects that are farther apart.

3. Permanent Magnets

Magnets have many shapes and sizes. Some magnets are round, and others look like a wand.

Most of the magnets you know are called *permanent magnets*. A **permanent magnet** is a magnet that you cannot turn on and off. They always pull with magnetic force. Some materials from Earth are magnetic. People use them to make permanent magnets.

Some permanent magnets are strong. Others are weak. A magnet's properties affect its magnetic force. For instance, magnets come in different sizes. Bigger magnets pull with a force stronger than smaller magnets of the same type.

Scientists and engineers often use permanent magnets. They can use them to separate metals from a mixture. They also use them in electronic devices like speakers.

One type of magnet is a permanent magnet. You cannot turn off its magnetic force.

Scientists and engineers study the properties of permanent magnets. A magnet's properties can tell them about the strength of its magnetic force.

These electromagnets can pick up metal when electricity flows through them, but they drop the metal when electricity stops flowing. This is because you can turn magnetic force in electromagnets on and off.

4. Electromagnets

Permanent magnets always pull with magnetic force, but not all magnets are permanent. Some magnets can turn on and off.

Another kind of magnet is an *electromagnet*. An **electromagnet** is a magnet that can turn on and off. When electricity flows through an electromagnet, it pulls with magnetic force. But it stops pulling when electricity stops flowing.

You can make an electromagnet. Wrap a wire around an iron nail. Then connect the wire to a battery. Electricity flows through the wire. It gives the wire and nail magnetic force. You can pick up paper clips with it. The magnet turns off if you stop the electricity. The paper clips fall down.

Doorbells and motors use electromagnets. They are also used in scrap yards to pick up and drop off metal.

5. Magnets and Technology

If you used a computer or watched television today, then you used a magnet. These devices and many others use magnets to work.

Engineers study how magnetic forces work. Using what they learn, engineers design tools that use magnets. One of these tools is a stepper motor. Naval ships once used big stepper motors to aim weapons. Today, small stepper motors are in electronics like computers and printers.

How do engineers use magnets to make a stepper motor spin? The motor has a ring made of electromagnets. Inside of the ring is a permanent magnet. Two electromagnets on opposite sides of the ring turn on, which makes unlike poles. They pull the permanent magnet, so it turns to line up with them. This causes the motor to spin.

Engineers use what they know about magnets to design a stepper motor. When electromagnets in the ring (right) turn on, the permanent magnet (left) that goes inside the ring spins.

This maglev train was designed using the steps that engineers follow. Engineers studied the properties of magnets to design this train.

⚙ *Engineering Design*

6. Solving Problems with Magnets

Did you know that some trains float above their tracks? They are called maglev trains.

Engineers use scientific knowledge to design objects. You can act like an engineer to design a maglev train. How can magnets cause a train to float? You know that like poles repel. You can test magnet poles to see if they can float a train.

Engineers make models of their designs. You decide to make a model of a train from cardboard. You put magnets under the train with the north poles facing down. You put magnets on the track with the north poles facing up.

Engineers test their models. You hold the train above the track, but it falls to the side. You need to change your design, so you put boards on both sides of the track. When you test your new design, the train floats in place.

What Can Magnetic Forces Do?

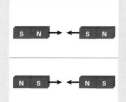

1. Magnetic Forces   Magnetic forces work between objects that do not touch. Every magnet has a north pole and a south pole. Unlike poles attract. Like poles repel.

2. Stronger and Weaker Magnetic Forces   Magnetic force is strongest near a magnet's poles and when objects are close together. It is weaker when objects are far apart.

3. Permanent Magnets   Most of the magnets you know are called permanent magnets. Magnetic force in permanent magnets cannot be turned off.

4. Electromagnets   Electricity gives electromagnets magnetic force. But electromagnets only work when electricity flows through them.

5. Magnets and Technology   Scientists study how magnets work. Engineers design technologies based on what they know about magnetic forces.

6. Solving Problems with Magnets   You can act like an engineer to design a maglev train using magnets. You can make and test a model of the design to see if it works.

Floating Trains

Engineers have been making trains better since the early 1800s. They have even found a way to make trains float! They do this by using electromagnets.

"All aboard!" calls the conductor. It's 1850, and your family is traveling by train for the first time. The heavy locomotive moves forward. It starts moving faster and faster until it reaches a speed of 24 kilometers per hour (15 miles per hour). You have never moved so fast!

The chugging of the engine is so loud that you almost have to shout to be heard. And walking from one train car to another is not easy. The train shakes, so you sway in the aisle.

The trains of the 1800s and early 1900s were steam trains. Burning coal changed water into steam, which powered the engine that pulled the train. Trains have changed a lot since then. Now they are much smoother, quieter, and faster!

Steam trains, like this one, were used in the 1800s and 1900s. They use steam to power their engines.

Power Up!

In the mid-1900s, engineers improved trains. They made diesel engines. Diesel is a fuel like gasoline. Engines that run on diesel are much more powerful than steam engines. They can move heavier trains than steam engines. They're also faster. Today's trains use diesel engines. They reach speeds of around 240 kilometers per hour (about 150 miles per hour).

Engineers also made the train cars more comfortable. They added air conditioning and heating. They reduced the shaking and noise of the train, too.

In the 1980s and 1990s, engineers improved trains even more. They designed high-speed electric trains. In 2007, an electric train in France reached a speed of nearly 575 kilometers per hour (357 miles per hour)! That's the fastest a train with wheels has ever gone!

Diesel trains are used all over the world. They are faster and longer than steam trains.

Floating on Air

The French train is the fastest train with wheels, but trains *without* wheels can go even faster. How can a train run without wheels? It floats, or *levitates,* by using electromagnets.

Trains that float are called maglev trains. The name is short for *magnetic levitation.* The magnets that make a train float do so by either repelling or attracting one another.

In the 1970s, Japanese engineers started working on a maglev train that floats. Both the train and the train tracks contain electromagnets. When both magnets are on, they repel each other. The repelling force pushes the train upward. The train floats about 10 cm (4 in) above the track.

Japanese engineers designed a maglev train similar to this one. It uses electromagnets to move.

More Attractive Floating

German engineers also worked on a maglev train around the same time as Japanese engineers. But this system worked differently.

The German system made the train float using an attractive magnetic force. The base of this train wraps around its train track. An electromagnet on the part of the train under the track is attracted to the metal track. This attractive force pulls the train up. But the train does not touch the rail. It just floats around it.

In 2003, a maglev train using the German system started running in China. It reaches speeds of up to 430 kilometers per hour (267 miles per hour)! Because the train floats on air, the ride is not bumpy. Since there is no engine, the train also does not make much noise. What a change from the old steam trains!

You can see how the base of a German maglev train wraps around the track.

What Can Electric Forces Do?

Why does this student's hair stand up after going down a slide? You will learn how electric forces can affect objects without touching them, even a person's hair. Electric forces can be strong or weak. You can produce some types of electricity. Electric forces can also be found in nature.

 NGSS **3-PS2-3.** Ask questions to determine cause and effect relationships of electric or magnetic interactions between two objects not in contact with each other.

PS2.B. Electric and magnetic forces between a pair of objects do not require that the objects be in contact. The sizes of the forces in each situation depend on the properties of the objects and their distances apart and, for forces between two magnets, on their orientation relative to each other.

Cause and Effect Cause and effect relationships are routinely identified, tested, and used to explain change.

 Asking Questions and Defining Problems

1. Electric Forces

You learned that magnetic forces can push or pull objects that do not touch. Another type of force, called *electric force*, can also do this.

Electric force is a push or pull between objects that have electric charges. Objects are covered in electric charges, but the charges are too small to see. These charges can build up in objects. When you go down a slide, electric charges stick to you and build up. When you brush your hair, electric charges build up in the hairbrush.

Electric charges can be *positive* (+) or *negative* (–). These charges act similarly to poles on a magnet. Unlike charges attract. A positive charge and a negative charge pull toward each other. Like charges repel. Two positive charges push away from each other. So do two negative charges.

Electric charges react to each other. Unlike charges attract, and like charges repel.

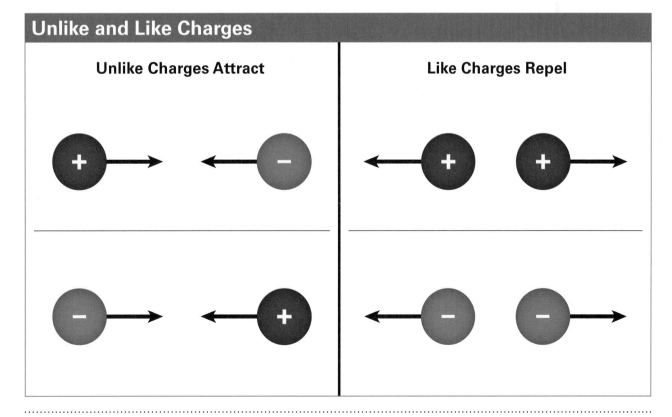

Unlike and Like Charges

Unlike Charges Attract

Like Charges Repel

Electric charges on this balloon are pulling the paper up. Electric force between objects is strong when they are close together.

2. Stronger and Weaker Electric Forces

Unlike charges pull toward each other. But like charges push away each other. When do electric forces pull or push the strongest?

Rub a balloon on your shirt. Electric charges from your shirt stick to the balloon. Then hold it just above pieces of paper. The paper stands up. This is because electric charges on the balloon are pulling on the paper. Like magnetic forces, electric forces are strong between objects that are close together.

What happens if you hold the balloon farther away? Rub a balloon on your shirt and hold it high above the paper. The paper does not move. This is because electric charges on the balloon are pulling with less strength. Like magnetic forces, electric forces are weaker between objects that are farther apart.

3. Static Electricity

If you unload a dryer, you might see two socks stuck together. You might even see a spark if you pull them apart. Why does this happen?

When clothes rub together in a dryer, electric charges build up on them. More of one type of charge may build up. An imbalance of positive and negative charges causes **static electricity**. You can produce static electricity. Slide your feet across carpet. Charges stick to you. You might see a spark if charges jump to an object.

Objects charged with static electricity can pull or push with electric force on another object. Rub a balloon on your hair. The balloon and your hair build up unlike charges. Pull the balloon up. Electric forces cause the balloon to lift your hair.

Rub two balloons on your hair. They get the same electric charge. Hang the balloons near each other. The like charges between the balloons push each other away.

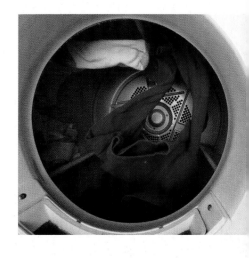

Electric charges buildup when clothes rub together in a dryer. This buildup is called static electricity.

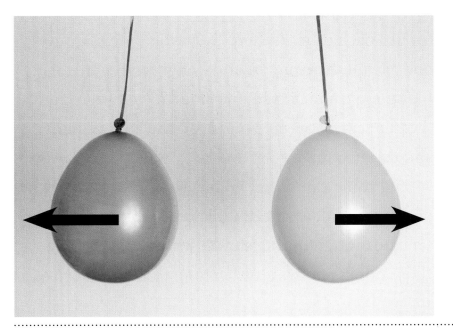

Static electricity between these balloons pushes them away from each other. The balloons have like electric charges, so they repel each other.

Unlike charges pull toward each other with such a strong force that a lightning strike jumps from the cloud to the ground. Lightning strikes are dangerous, so stay indoors during a lightning storm.

4. Electric Forces in Nature

During a storm, you might have seen lightning flash in the sky. Why does this happen?

Strong electric forces cause lightning. It starts with the buildup of lots of electric charges in the clouds. Positive charges gather in some parts of a cloud. Negative charges gather in other parts. When these buildups of unlike charges attract, they pull toward each other. When the charges jump from one part of the cloud to another, lightning occurs. Lightning can occur in one cloud or between clouds. It can occur between clouds and the air or clouds and the ground.

Lightning can be very dangerous. It can cause fires on the ground, and it can kill living things. To stay safe during a lightning storm, stay indoors or in a car. Close doors and windows. Avoid electrical devices.

What Can Electric Forces Do?

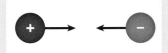
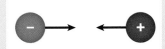

1. Electric Forces   Objects are covered in electric charges that are too small to see. The charges may be positive or negative and can build up in objects. Electric forces between these objects can push or pull them even if they do not touch. Objects with unlike charges attract, while objects with like charges repel.

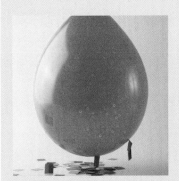

2. Stronger and Weaker Electric Forces   Electric forces can be strong or weak between objects. An electric force between objects is stronger when the objects are closer together. The force is weaker between objects when the objects are farther apart.

3. Static Electricity   Static electricity is caused by an imbalance of positive or negative charges on an object. More of one type of electric charge can build on an object when objects rub together. Static electricity can be strong enough to move objects without touching them.

4. Electric Forces in Nature   During a storm, positive and negative electric charges can build up in different parts of a cloud. When the charges attract, lightning occurs. Lightning can be dangerous, so it is best to stay indoors during a lightning storm.

Electricity in Nature

Lightning flashes! It is as if electric sparks have lit up the dark night sky. Lightning does not just look like electricity. Lightning *is* electricity! What other kinds of electricity can you find in nature?

Picture sailing through a storm in the 1600s. You see a blue glow and sparks at the top of the ship's mast. But as the soon as the storm clears, the light goes away and leaves no trace.

Sailors named the glowing blue fire that appeared on ships' masts St. Elmo's fire. For centuries, people observed St. Elmo's fire without knowing what it is. But, thanks to science, we now know that St. Elmo's fire happens when air becomes electrically charged. As the air becomes charged, it glows and sparks. The glow of St. Elmo's fire is the same as the glow from a neon light. You could even say that a neon light is St. Elmo's fire in a tube!

The blue glow in this ball is similar to St. Elmo's fire. In the 1600s, sailors used to see St. Elmo's fire on the mast of their ships.

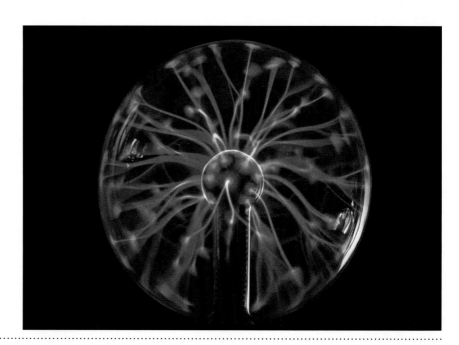

Lights in the Sky

St. Elmo's fire is not the only electric light that occurs in nature. *Auroras* are blue, green, or red streaks of light that appear in the night sky. You can see them near Earth's poles.

People in different parts of the world have explained auroras in different ways. In Finland, people thought a fox caused auroras by sweeping snow up into the sky. Eskimos thought auroras were spirits dancing. Some people saw auroras as a sign of good luck. Others thought they meant bad things would happen.

Scientists learned that auroras are caused when charged pieces of matter from the sun hit the air around Earth. The air becomes charged and starts to glow. In this way, auroras are similar to St. Elmo's fire.

Auroras are streaks of color in the sky. They move around like curtains in the wind.

Shocking!

St. Elmo's fire and auroras are examples of electricity in the sky. But electricity occurs in other places in nature. An electric eel is a kind of fish that uses electricity! An electric eel can build up a huge electric charge. It uses this electricity to shock animals that it wants to eat. It also uses it to scare away animals.

Electric eels make electricity in special body parts. Thousands of these parts are lined up like batteries in a flashlight. Scientists think they can imitate the way eels make electricity. Scientists hope that making electricity in this way can power small machines that are used in medicine. Imagine having a machine in your body that keeps you alive with electric eel power!

Electric eels make electricity to shock other living things.

An echidna senses electricity with its nose.

Even More Shocking!

Many other animals make or use electricity. Like electric eels, a lot of electric animals live in water. This is because electricity can travel easily through water. One such creature is the funny-shaped elephant nose fish. It also uses electricity to hunt and avoid its enemies.

Some electric animals live on land. An echidna is a small animal that lives in Australia. Part of an echidna's nose can sense electricity. Scientists think echidnas use this sense to find food. But they are still not sure how it works.

Perhaps the strangest electric animal is the oriental hornet. This insect can change light into electricity. Scientists know how the hornets make electricity but not how they use it. Let's hope that finding out isn't too big of a shock!

An oriental hornet changes light into electricity, but no one knows why!

UNIT 3
Weather and Climate

It's nighttime and rain is falling hard on the roof. This is unusual in your desert town. Suddenly you see lightning in the night sky. You count, "One one-thousand, two one-thousand," then bang! You hear thunder. It's so close. What causes these thunderstorms? In this unit, you will learn about different types of weather and how scientists study them.

Unit Contents

Unit 3 Overview

Graphic Organizer: This unit is structured to introduce **weather**, teach the ways scientists **gather weather data**, describe how that data are used, and illuminate the challenges posed by extreme weather.

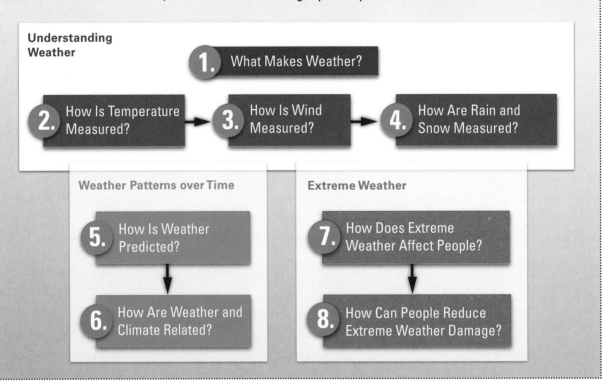

Understanding Weather

1. What Makes Weather?

2. How Is Temperature Measured?

3. How Is Wind Measured?

4. How Are Rain and Snow Measured?

Weather Patterns over Time

5. How Is Weather Predicted?

6. How Are Weather and Climate Related?

Extreme Weather

7. How Does Extreme Weather Affect People?

8. How Can People Reduce Extreme Weather Damage?

NGSS Next Generation Science Standards

Performance Expectations

3-ESS2-1. Represent data in tables and graphical displays to describe typical weather conditions expected during a particular season.

3-ESS2-2. Obtain and combine information to describe climates in different regions of the world.

3-ESS3-1. Make a claim about the merit of a design solution that reduces the impacts of a weather-related hazard.

Disciplinary Core Ideas

ESS2.D: Weather and Climate

- Scientists record patterns of the weather across different times and areas so that they can make predictions about what kind of weather might happen next.

- Climate describes a range of an area's typical weather conditions and the extent to which those conditions vary over years.

ESS3.B: Natural Hazards

- A variety of natural hazards result from natural processes. Humans cannot eliminate natural hazards but can take steps to reduce their impacts.

Crosscutting Concepts

Patterns

- Patterns of change can be used to make predictions.

Cause and Effect

- Cause and effect relationships are routinely identified, tested, and used to explain change.

 Analyzing and Interpreting Data

 Engaging in Argument from Evidence

 Obtaining, Evaluation, and Communicating Information

Have you ever wondered...

If you observe the weather where you live, you will notice that it changes. This unit will help you answer these questions and many others you may ask.

How do you measure rain?

What causes wind?

Why is it cooler in the shade than it is in the sun?

What Makes Weather?

Science Vocabulary

atmosphere

humidity

temperature

water vapor

weather

Weather happens all around you. What does it mean when someone says that the weather will be rainy or warm? Some places tend to have one kind of weather or another. But weather is always changing. These changes can happen in patterns that scientists study. The patterns help predict the weather in different areas.

NGSS

3-ESS2-1. Represent data in tables and graphical displays to describe typical weather conditions expected during a particular season.

ESS2.D. Scientists record patterns of the weather across different times and areas so that they can make predictions about what kind of weather might happen next.

Patterns Patterns of change can be used to make predictions.

Analyzing and Interpreting Data

1. Weather Changes

You can plan your day better if you know what the *weather* will be like. If it is rainy or cold, then you might carry an umbrella or wear a jacket. But the weather can change. It can be rainy and cool, then warm and sunny an hour later. How does weather change? Where does it happen?

The **atmosphere** is the blanket of air that surrounds Earth. The atmosphere is made up of layers. The highest layer is farthest from Earth's surface. The layer closest to Earth's surface is where most types of weather occur.

Weather is what the atmosphere is like at a certain time and place. Weather changes from day to day and hour to hour. Weather has many parts—air temperature, wind, and the amount of water in the air. These parts create the type of weather you see and feel.

The atmosphere has several layers. Weather happens in the layer of the atmosphere that is closest to Earth.

One part of weather is the air's temperature. At the beach it may be warm enough to wear shorts.

2. Temperature and Weather

Is it too warm for a sweater? Is it cold enough to wear gloves? These are some questions you may ask when thinking about how the air feels.

One part of weather is the air's *temperature*. **Temperature** is how warm or cool something is. Different places tend to have temperature patterns. Some places are hot. In Miami, Florida, the weather is often warm enough to wear shorts during winter. In summer, it gets hotter there. In Chicago, Illinois, the weather is often very cold in winter. You usually need to wear a coat, hat, and mittens.

Air temperature can change quickly or slowly. A late spring morning can feel cool, so you wear long pants. But by noon, it feels hot, so you change into shorts. It may be warm enough to swim. When the sun sets, air temperature can cool down.

When the sun sets, the air gets cooler. People dress to keep warm.

3. Wind and Weather

Think about a flag hanging on a pole outdoors. On a windy day, would the flag look different than on a day the wind was not blowing?

Another part of weather is wind. Air in Earth's atmosphere is always moving. You feel this as wind. Wind moves across Earth's surface. Some winds only blow for a short distance or time. Other winds blow around the whole world.

Wind can be slow or fast. Sometimes air feels still, as if it is not moving at all. On a windy day, you can feel air pushing against you. A light wind can move tree leaves and other light objects. You may see a flag wave in a soft breeze. A faster, stronger wind can blow a hat off your head, lift kites, or push sailboats. Sometimes winds are fast enough to knock down trees or tear parts off a roof.

The wind can power windmills, cause waves to form, and blow down trees.

Windy days allow for some activities like windsurfing.

Water is in the air in the form of clouds and rain. It is also in the air in the form of water vapor, which you cannot see.

4. Water and Weather

Have you ever thought the air outdoors felt wet? Why does the air feel that way?

An important part of weather is the amount of water in the air. The layer of the atmosphere closest to Earth contains water in different forms. One form of water in the air is *water vapor*. **Water vapor** is water in the air that you cannot see. Wetness you feel in the air when it is not raining or foggy is due to water vapor. **Humidity** is the amount of water vapor in the air.

Water is also in the air in the form of clouds. Tiny droplets of water collect and form shapes you see as clouds. You may see white clouds on a sunny day. You have probably seen dark clouds on a rainy day. Water that becomes too large to float falls in the form of rain or snow.

What Makes Weather?

1. Weather Changes   The atmosphere is a blanket of air around Earth. Weather is the state of the atmosphere at a certain time and place. The weather is changing all the time. It gets cooler or warmer, drier or wetter, calmer or windier. There are many parts to weather.

2. Temperature and Weather   One part of weather is the temperature of the air. Temperature is how warm or cool something is. The air's temperature changes during the day and over the course of the year. Different places tend to have certain kinds of temperature patterns.

3. Wind and Weather   Another part of weather is the wind. Wind is the moving air in Earth's atmosphere. Some winds are slow, and others are fast. Different speeds of wind have different effects. Very fast, strong winds can cause damage.

4. Water and Weather   Another part of weather has to do with water. Water in the atmosphere is in different forms. Some of it cannot be seen. This is called water vapor. Sometimes water vapor forms droplets of water in clouds. Later it turns into rain or snow.

Weather Superheroes

Powerful hurricanes can destroy whole towns. People can stay safe if they leave before the storm arrives. Who are the superheroes who decide when it is time to evacuate ahead of a storm?

The family watched in horror as the windows shattered. Ocean water poured in, flooding the cellar. The rising water knocked out the electric power. They rushed upstairs in the pitch-dark as the water swiftly rose behind them.

The family had chosen to stay in their home during Hurricane Sandy in Queens, New York, in October 2012. The weather forecasters had warned everyone to evacuate before the storm hit. But, just the year before, they were told the same thing. When last year's hurricane finally hit shore, nothing much had happened. So, this year, they had decided to stay put. As you will see, this would prove to be a big mistake!

Most people who left before Hurricane Sandy hit were safe. The storm destroyed many homes, like this one.

As the scientist in charge of a National Weather Service office in New Jersey, Gary Szatkowski knows he must consider his words carefully when he writes storm warnings.

A Superhero Saves the Day

How could this family and others know when to evacuate? They must rely on scientists who have to make very hard decisions. Gary Szatkowski is one such scientist. He has to be very careful when he sends a weather warning. If he says a storm will be dangerous and it is not, people might not listen the next time.

Six days before Hurricane Sandy hit land, most computer models showed the storm going safely out to sea. But Szatkowski thought it would take a different path. He predicted it would hit the coasts of New York, New Jersey, and Connecticut. And he thought it would hit hard. Millions of people were in danger.

Szatkowski was scared he was wrong. But he was more scared that he was right. He sent the strongest warnings he had ever written. And by doing so, he saved hundreds of lives.

Radar towers, like this one, help show where rain is heaviest.

Powerful computers help make forecasts. Weather heroes must be able to work well with people, too.

Using His Superpowers

Lifesaving heroes like Szatkowski have special tools to help them do their jobs. They use satellites, radar, and other tools to gather data. They program computers to analyze the data. Then they can make forecasts from computer models.

But an accurate forecast does no good if people do not understand the danger it predicts. To save lives, a weather superhero must be able to convince people. Without this ability, people may not believe a storm is dangerous. So, they might not leave their homes for safer shelter.

Szatkowski knew Hurricane Sandy was going to be the worst storm ever seen in that area. He also knew that some people still had not evacuated. The day before the storm hit, he decided to use a weather expert's most powerful form of persuasion. He would beg.

Szatkowski made a personal plea begging everyone to flee. "If you think the storm is over-hyped . . . please err on the side of caution," he wrote. He invited people to blame him if they ended up leaving home needlessly. "You can . . . yell at me all you want," he wrote. " . . . I will be very happy that you are alive & well, no matter how much you yell at me."

The family in Queens who did not listen to the superhero's warning? Luckily, no one was hurt. But the storm destroyed the family's cars. It flooded the home's first floor. Nearby houses exploded when water caused wires to spark and set fire to gas lines. "I wish I had evacuated," one member said. "There was a point there where it was so scary that I looked at my family and said, 'What have I done?'"

Queens, New York, was still in ruins months after Hurricane Sandy.

How Is Temperature Measured?

Science Vocabulary

thermometer

weather station

Why are some places on Earth very cold and others very warm? The sun is the source of almost all the heat on Earth's surface. But the sun heats different places different amounts. People have tools to find out how warm it is at different times and places on Earth.

3-ESS2-1. Represent data in tables and graphical displays to describe typical weather conditions expected during a particular season.

ESS2.D. Scientists record patterns of the weather across different times and areas so that they can make predictions about what kind of weather might happen next.

Patterns Patterns of change can be used to make predictions.

Analyzing and Interpreting Data

1. The Sun Heats Earth's Surface

Have you noticed on a warm day that it feels cooler in the shade? What causes air temperature to change?

Recall that temperature is how warm or cold something is. You can measure the temperature of water, air, and other materials. You can even measure the temperature of your body! Part of weather is the air's temperature.

The sun causes air temperature on Earth to change. Earth's surface is heated by the sun. The sun's energy heats the ground, and the ground warms the air above it. The air is also heated a little bit directly by the sun. The sun heats Earth more in some places than others. This causes some places to be warm and other places to be cool. Air temperature changes daily, hourly, or from minute to minute.

The sun heats Earth's surface, but not evenly. During the day, the temperature in this meadow will be warmer than under the shade of the trees.

Spring thermometers, like this one, have parts that sense heat and move a dial.

This bulb thermometer shows both °C and °F. The numbers are different but the temperature is the same.

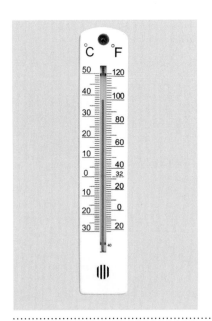

2. Measuring Temperature

You check the weather report. What does temperature tell you about weather?

A **thermometer** is a tool that measures temperature. There are different ways to say what the temperature is, called *temperature scales*. In the United States, most weather reports use °F, or "degrees Fahrenheit." In most other parts of the world °C, or "degrees Celsius," is used.

Both scales measure the same temperature, but they use different numbers. For example, the temperature at which water freezes is called 0°C. But it is also called 32°F. So, 0°C and 32°F are the same temperature. The temperature at which water boils is 100°C or 212°F. So, 100°C and 212°F are the same temperature. You have to say which scale you are using. Otherwise people will not know what the temperature means.

Kinds of Thermometers

There are different kinds of thermometers. A bulb thermometer has a clear tube filled with liquid. When the liquid warms up, it takes up more space and rises. A spring thermometer works in a similar way. Instead of using liquid, it has a metal part inside that gets larger and smaller. These changes move a pointer. The pointer shows the temperature.

Ways Thermometers Are Helpful

Thermometers show how hot or cold something is. They help you plan. If a thermometer reads 13°C (55°F), the air feels cool. You may need a jacket.

A thermometer is one of the tools in a *weather station*. **Weather stations** have equipment that measure temperature and other weather-related information. They normally measure it many times a day. The measurements can reveal patterns used to predict weather. This information is sent to newspapers, television stations, and the Internet.

Weather stations have equipment that measure temperature and other weather information.

Temperature data from weather stations are sent to other places for people to use. This lets people quickly learn about temperatures almost everywhere on Earth.

3. Temperature Patterns

Temperatures are higher during the day and lower at night. During the day, the sun's energy heats Earth's surface. This includes rocks, roads, buildings, even lakes and the ocean. Earth's surface heats the air above it. Each night when the sun sets, Earth's surface stops being heated. The air cools down. Each day and night, this pattern of warm and cool temperatures repeats.

Seasons also have patterns of warmer and cooler temperatures. There are four seasons. Summer has the warmest temperatures. In fall, temperatures begin to cool. The air is coldest during winter. In spring, the air gets warmer again. The pattern repeats. Temperature patterns are different in different places. Florida has a pattern of mild winters. Maine has a pattern of very cold winters.

Air temperatures have a pattern of being warmer during the day and colder at night. Air temperature also has seasonal patterns.

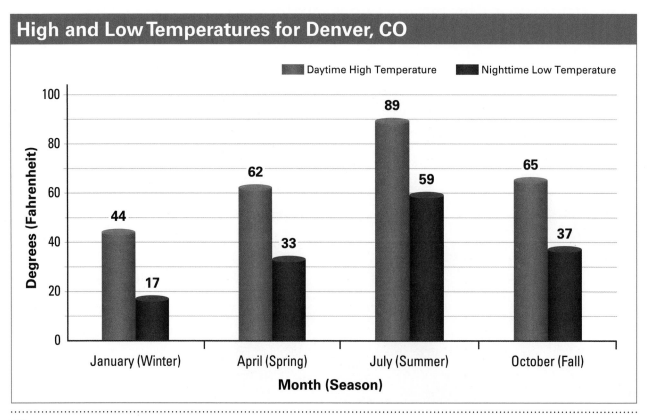

High and Low Temperatures for Denver, CO

How Is Temperature Measured?

1. The Sun Heats Earth's Surface During the day, the sun's rays heat the ground at Earth's surface. Then the ground heats the air above it. This causes the air's temperature to rise. Air temperatures vary across Earth's surface. This is because the sun heats some places more than others. Air temperatures are always changing.

2. Measuring Temperature Tools called thermometers are used to measure temperatures. There are different kinds of thermometers. Temperature is measured on two different scales, Celsius and Fahrenheit. It is useful to know what the temperature is in different places. So, weather stations take the air's temperature all over the world.

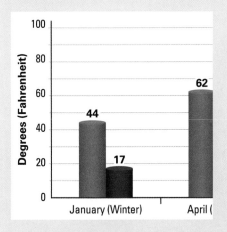

3. Temperature Patterns There are patterns in the way temperatures change. Air temperatures tend to be warmer during the day and cooler at night. This cycle repeats almost every day. There are also patterns in the seasons. Much of the United States has hot summers and cold winters. Different places have different patterns.

Too Hot, Too Cold!

Do you remember a time when it was really hot or cold outside for days? Temperature extremes can cause big problems. They can even be deadly.

It was still morning, but the heat was already bad, even for July. The mail carrier had miles of walking ahead of him. He knew the heat could make him very ill. It could even land him in the hospital. So, he drank cold water from his water bottle. Then he poured some water over his head.

Part of a mail carrier's job is staying safe in the heat. But many people get caught by surprise. During a heat wave, people who work outside sometimes do not drink enough water and end up in the emergency room. This is because if you do not drink enough water, you can get heat exhaustion. This means that your body cannot cool itself, so your temperature rises.

Water can help you stay well during a heat wave. Drink some first, and then use it to cool off.

Heat Waves

Do you think you're safe during a heat wave if you stay indoors? Watch out. You can still get sick inside if you are not used to the heat. If your house is too hot, find out if your city has any cooling centers. Some are air-conditioned buildings, like libraries. Others are outdoor fountains or open fire hydrants. There, you can cool down by getting wet.

Heat waves can also harm nonliving things. Engineers build spaces into bridges and roads so that they can expand when it is very hot. But heat waves are sometimes hotter than engineers planned for. At times like this, the heat bends railroads. It can cause bridges to sag. Bridges and roads must be fixed right away to avoid accidents. Sometimes, pavement even explodes during a heat wave!

Heat waves can bend rails and explode pavement.

Cold Snaps

The heat wave is finally over. The air is cool and crisp. Wait . . . now it is cold—too cold! A cold snap happens when the temperature is unusually cold for days on end. Cold snaps in winter can be as risky as heat waves in summer.

One serious way that cold can hurt you is frostbite. Frostbite happens when a body part gets so cold it freezes. People can lose fingers, toes, or even noses from really bad cases of frostbite. But, if you dress warmly and watch for the warning signs, you can stay safe.

If your skin turns red and feels either cold or hot, you may have frostnip. Frostnip is the beginning stage of frostbite. If you get frostnip, cover the skin with warm, dry clothing and get indoors. Gently warm your skin in warm, not hot, water. And next time you go out, bundle up!

You can prevent frostnip and frostbite by covering as much of your skin as possible when you go out in the cold.

Hypothermia

Another way that cold can hurt you is hypothermia. Hypothermia happens when you are cold for so long that your body cannot keep warm enough. If you are wet in the cold, you can get sick quickly. This is because wet skin loses a lot of heat. You know you are too cold if you start to shiver. Shivering is your body's way to warm itself. It is also a sign that you need to get warm and dry as soon as possible.

Cold snaps do not just hurt people. They can also damage plants. You can see the results at the grocery store. A cold snap in Florida can kill crops like oranges. You might still see those foods at the store. But they will be scarce and expensive.

If your area is experiencing temperature extremes, it can be uncomfortable. But hang in there. Soon, it will get back to normal.

People can go indoors to warm up during a cold snap. Crops, like these oranges, are stuck outside in the freezing cold.

How Is Wind Measured?

Science Vocabulary

anemometer

wind vane

You cannot see the wind. But you still know it exists. Have you ever had a gust of wind blow something away so you had to run after it? The wind is a part of weather. The speed of wind can be measured. The wind can occur in patterns that can be predicted. Scientists study the wind with special tools.

NGSS

3-ESS2-1. Represent data in tables and graphical displays to describe typical weather conditions expected during a particular season.

ESS2.D. Scientists record patterns of the weather across different times and areas so that they can make predictions about what kind of weather might happen next.

Patterns Patterns of change can be used to make predictions.

Analyzing and Interpreting Data

1. The Sun and Wind

You have probably felt a breeze blowing across your skin or seen tree branches bending during a storm. What causes wind?

Recall that the sun's energy heats Earth's surface. But it doesn't heat the ground evenly. Some places are sunnier than others. Shadows from clouds can cool an area. Warm air is lighter than cool air. So, it rises. Cooler air sinks or stays low. When warm air rises, cooler air moves in from the sides to take its place. The air in different places is always heating up or cooling down, which means it is always moving. This movement of air is the wind.

The force of the wind pushes on and moves objects. You see this when leaves blow or flags flap. You can feel the force of wind on your skin on a breezy day.

The air is constantly heating up and cooling down, which means that air is always on the move. This motion of the air is called wind.

How Wind Forms

Warm air

Cool air

This tool is called an anemometer. It uses spinning cups to measure the speed of the wind.

2. Measuring Wind Speed

A storm can bring fast, strong winds. How do you know how fast the winds move?

Wind can be described by its speed, or how fast it is moving. An **anemometer** is a tool that measures wind speed. Some use cups attached to rods. Wind pushes the cups, and the rods turn. They turn faster if the wind is stronger. In the United States, wind speed is measured in miles per hour (mph). In other places around the world, speed is measured in kilometers per hour (km/h). The speed is the same, but the numbers are different.

Winds with different speeds are called different things. If the wind speed is slow, you feel a gentle breeze. If the wind is fast, large tree branches start bending. Winds that blow during hurricanes are very fast and strong. They can damage buildings or uproot trees. The faster the wind, the stronger it is.

The faster winds blow, the stronger the effects they have. Strong winds affect people and objects.

The arrow of a wind vane points in the direction the wind is coming from. This is the opposite of the way a windsock points.

3. Measuring Wind Direction

If you see a storm in the distance, will it come your way? Knowing how the wind is blowing might help.

A **wind vane** is a weather tool that shows the direction the wind is blowing from. On a wind vane, a pointer is attached to a pole. The pointer moves with the wind. The arrow points in the direction the wind is coming from. Winds are described by the direction they come from, not the direction they are headed. If the arrow points to the west, the wind is a west wind, or a wind coming from the west.

Windsocks show wind direction, too. A windsock is a cloth tube attached to a pole. When the wind blows, the narrow end of the sock goes downwind. So, the windsock points in the direction that wind is blowing. The pole stays on the side the wind is coming from. Windsocks also give an idea of how fast, or strong, the wind is.

A windsock shows the direction the wind is blowing and how strong it is. Windsocks can be seen from far away.

4. Wind Patterns

Wind patterns depend on changes in the air temperature. Winds often blow from cool areas to warm areas. Near the ocean, land is warm during the day. Cool breezes blow from the cool ocean onto land. At night, the land cools and the ocean is warmer. Cool breezes blow from land to the ocean.

Some wind patterns happen during certain times of the year. The Santa Anas are dry, dusty winds that blow in southern California. They blow from east to west, from the deserts to the ocean. The Santa Anas blow each year from fall to spring.

Different places on Earth have different wind patterns. Some winds blow across large areas of Earth's surface. Westerlies are winds that move from west to east. Westerlies blow across much of the United States. Easterlies, or Trade Winds, are winds that blow from east to west in warm, tropical areas.

During the day, cool winds blow from the water onto land. At night, cool winds blow from the land out over the ocean.

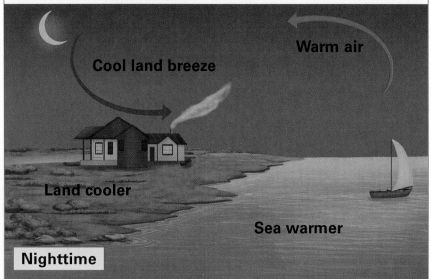

How Sea Breezes Form

Warm air

Cool sea breeze

Land warmer

Sea cooler

Daytime

Cool land breeze

Warm air

Land cooler

Sea warmer

Nighttime

How Is Wind Measured?

1. The Sun and Wind   The sun causes changes in temperature. These different temperatures cause wind. Warmer, lighter air in the atmosphere tends to rise. Cooler, heavier air moves in from below to take its place. The movement of all this air is wind.

2. Measuring Wind Speed   The speed of the wind affects how strong it is. Just as thermometers measure temperature, a device called an anemometer measures wind speed. The faster the wind moves, the stronger it is. Strong winds can be dangerous.

3. Measuring Wind Direction   Winds can be described by the direction they blow. When people talk about the wind direction, they mean the direction the wind is coming from. Wind vanes and windsocks are different kinds of tools. They both show the wind's direction.

4. Wind Patterns   Just like temperatures, winds have patterns. Winds normally blow from cool areas to warmer areas. Some wind patterns are specific to a place. Ocean breezes blow onto land during the day and out to sea at night. Other wind patterns blow around the world.

Big City Weather

If you live in a city, you need different clothes than you would if you lived in the countryside. One reason for this is that cities have different weather than the surrounding countryside. How can that be?

José was homesick and hot. "Look at the temperature—it's ninety-seven degrees! I'm tired of trees and grass. I want buildings and pavement. I'm asking Gramp to drive us home."

"Oh, no, you're not," his sister said. "I like staying on Gramp's farm for the summer. Besides, it will only be hotter back home in the city." She texted their father to ask for proof and then showed José the answer. "See?"

"A hundred and four degrees!" José moaned. "How can it possibly be hotter in the city? It's only an hour away." José may not realize it, but cities are warmer, wetter, and windier than the nearby areas around them.

Cities are often warmer than nearby areas in the countryside.

Urban Heat Islands

Cities are hotter than the countryside because cities change the weather just by being there. This is how it works.

The sun heats Earth's surface. Dark surfaces heat faster than light ones. Dry surfaces also heat faster than wet ones. Cities are full of dark surfaces that dry quickly, like streets and brick buildings. When the warm sunlight hits them, city temperatures rise quickly.

Meanwhile, out in the countryside, lighter-colored grass and trees reflect more sunlight. All those plants give off moisture from water that soaked into the soil. The temperature rises there. But not as much as in the city.

Scientists call cities "urban heat islands." This is because a city's higher temperatures stand out like an island in a sea of cool.

When the sun hits surfaces like streets, a city heats up. This is one reason why cities are warmer than the country.

Growing plants or painting roofs white are both good ways to help cool urban heat islands.

Cooling the Islands

Luckily there are ways to keep cities cooler. One way is to cover more city surfaces with plants. Parks, gardens, and even a few trees between the sidewalk and street can make a difference. But a city has more buildings than parks. What can you do?

You can plant a park on top of a building! Many cities now want builders to put in "green roofs." Live plants on the roofs hold rainfall and reflect sunlight. This makes the city cooler. Buildings with green roofs need less air conditioning. So, owners save money, too.

Another way to cool a rooftop is to paint it white. The NYC °CoolRoofs program in New York City does what its name says. Volunteers paint dark roofs with a special white coating. The white roof reflects sunlight, and both the building and the city are cooler.

City Rain, City Wind

Cities don't just make it hotter. They also make it rainier. Buildings and pavement heat the air, and it rises. Any moisture in the air goes with it. Above the city, the air cools again. The moisture condenses into clouds above the city. Some of the clouds bring extra rain.

Windiness is another city weather quirk. Chicago's nickname is "The Windy City," but other cities are windy, too. This is because moving air speeds up when it goes around a building. Skyscrapers turn gentle breezes into big blasts down city streets. Scientists call what results the "urban wind tunnel" effect.

Some cities have put up buildings that use wind turbines. The turbines turn city wind into electric power. Cities may not be able to change the weather, but people can at least figure out how to put city weather to good use.

Cities are often very windy because buildings cause wind to move faster. Some cities have put wind turbines on buildings to turn wind into electric power.

How Are Rain and Snow Measured?

Science Vocabulary

drought

evaporation

precipitation

radar

rain gauge

Have you ever been caught in a heavy rainstorm? Or you might remember a time that it did not rain for a long time. The rain and snow that fall affect people in big ways. Scientists can measure rain and snow. They use the measurements to help predict weather.

 NGSS **3-ESS2-1.** Represent data in tables and graphical displays to describe typical weather conditions expected during a particular season.

ESS2.D. Scientists record patterns of the weather across different times and areas so that they can make predictions about what kind of weather might happen next.

Patterns Patterns of change can be used to make predictions.

 **Analyzing and Interpreting Data**

1. Water in the Air

You learned that water is in the air. Where does water in the air come from?

After a rainstorm there are puddles on the ground. Then these puddles dry up. Where did the water go? The liquid water in the puddle became water vapor. **Evaporation** is when liquid water turns to water vapor. The water vapor becomes part of the air. This is where humidity comes from!

Condensation happens when water vapor cools and changes back to liquid water. You may have seen this as dew on the grass. Clouds form the same way, but up in the air. The vapor changes to tiny liquid or frozen droplets you see as clouds. After a while, the droplets combine and get bigger. When the droplets become too heavy, they fall as *precipitation*. **Precipitation** is water that falls to the ground as rain, snow, or sleet.

When very humid air cools down, water vapor condenses into water droplets. You can see these water droplets on leaves and other objects.

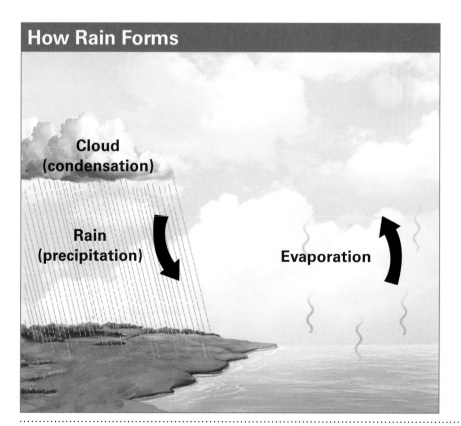

How Rain Forms

Cloud (condensation)

Rain (precipitation)

Evaporation

Heating or cooling water can cause it to change. This is what causes rain and snow.

2. Types of Precipitation

Suppose you see dark clouds on the horizon. What kind of precipitation will the clouds bring? Precipitation falls in many different forms.

Rain is precipitation that falls as a liquid. Water droplets and ice crystals form in clouds high in the atmosphere, where the air is cool. Ice is a solid form of water. When the droplets get too heavy, they cannot float in the air anymore. So, they fall. If the air near the ground is warm, these droplets fall as rain.

When the air near the ground is cold, precipitation can fall as snow or other forms. If the air is colder than 0°C (32°F), the ice crystals from the clouds stay frozen and fall as snow. But sometimes snow will start to melt on the way down. Then, if the air near the ground is colder than 0°C (32°F), the drops can freeze again into solid pieces called *sleet*. Sleet is frozen rain drops, or little ice pellets.

Rain, snow, and sleet are different types of precipitation. The type of precipitation that forms depends on the temperature.

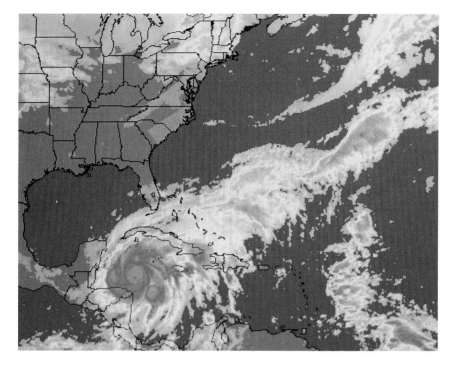

Weather radar can track storms. Radar maps show what kinds of precipitation are falling and how hard.

3. Measuring Precipitation

Sometimes the amount of rainfall is heavy. Other times the rain is a light sprinkle. It might rain for a long time or only for a few minutes.

You can use a *rain gauge* to measure how much rain fell. A **rain gauge** is a tool that measures rainfall. It has a container that collects rain. The tool shows how much rain has fallen during a period of time. Most rain gauges measure water in centimeters (cm), millimeters (mm), or inches (in).

Snow can be measured with a ruler. The ruler shows the depth of snow in inches or centimeters. *Radar* can also be used to find out about precipitation. **Radar** is a tool that is used to find far away objects in the air. Radar can also find the distance and speed of objects. Some weather stations use radar to track precipitation. Radar shows the kind of precipitation and how hard it is falling.

Rain gauges collect and measure rainfall during a period of time.

4. Precipitation Patterns

Some areas have rainy summers. Other areas are dry. Do all places get the same amount of rain?

Places have different precipitation patterns. Winters bring lots of snow to some places. Other areas have warmer, rainy winters. Some places have very rainy summers. In parts of Florida it can rain for a short time almost every summer day.

Some places receive very little rain. The Atacama Desert in Chile is the driest place on Earth. At the desert's center, there may not have been any rainfall for hundreds of years. Other places are very wet, like Hawaii. One mountain there gets more than 1143 cm (450 in) of rain each year.

Sometimes an area gets a different amount of rain than it is used to getting. **Drought** happens when not enough rain falls for a long period of time. Drought can happen in wet or dry regions.

Some deserts, like the Atacama in South America, are dry all year long. Other parts of Earth's surface get far more rain, like this mountain in Hawaii.

How Are Rain and Snow Measured?

1. Water in the Air   Water in the air has different forms. When liquid water on the ground evaporates, it goes into the air as water vapor. Water vapor can condense in the sky as clouds. The water eventually falls as precipitation, such as rain.

2. Types of Precipitation   Different forms of precipitation fall from clouds. Droplets of liquid water and ice in the clouds get too heavy. They fall to the ground. The form that falls as drops of liquid is called rain. When the air near the ground is colder, the water falls as snow or sleet.

3. Measuring Precipitation   Precipitation can be measured. A rain gauge is a simple tool that measures how much rain has fallen. The amount of snowfall can be measured with a ruler. Radar is a tool that lets people see how much precipitation is falling from far away.

4. Precipitation Patterns   Precipitation falls in patterns. Some times of the year tend to be wetter or drier than other times. There are other patterns of where rain falls. Places called deserts have patterns of very little precipitation. Other places are much wetter.

The Driest Place on Earth

Rainfall is rare in a desert, so water is scarce. Yet, many people choose to live in deserts. How do they survive?

Movie director Marc Forster looked out over the dry, bare landscape. No plants grew in the bare, red ground. No animals passed by—not even insects. It had not rained in years. "Yes," he thought. This was the perfect place to build the villain's hideout in his next movie.

Forster was visiting the Atacama Desert in the country of Chile. Chile stretches for more than half the length of the continent of South America. The Atacama Desert is the driest place on Earth. Less than half an inch of rain falls every hundred years. Very few plants or animals can live in a place this dry. This makes it a great spot for a movie villain to hide.

Years can go by without any rainfall in the Atacama Desert.

Bringing the Desert to Life

The Atacama Desert is too dry for almost any living thing to survive naturally. And yet, more than a million people live there. There are even cities, such as Iquique, in the Atacama Desert. People who live there need water every day for drinking, bathing, and cooking. How is it possible for them to make the desert home? They can live there because they bring water into the desert.

People have discovered several different ways to get water into the Atacama Desert. Long pipelines carry fresh water from distant mountains to cities on the coastline hundreds of miles away. Farmers drill wells to get at groundwater. They use the water for crops, such as grapes. In some villages, people buy water for everyday use from tanker trucks. But water from a truck is not cheap!

Pipelines carry fresh water from the mountains to the cities.

Iquique is a city in the Atacama Desert. People who live there cannot use salt water from the ocean.

There is fog in the Atacama Desert. Giant nets like this one are used to capture water from fog.

Catching Clouds

The Atacama Desert does not have rain. But it does have fog, which is another form of water. In some months, thick fog rolls across the desert. Fog is a cloud. It is made up of tiny droplets of water floating in air.

People have found a way to capture fog and drink it. They string up huge nets made of cheap materials along hilltops. As fog rolls through the nets, water drops gather on the nets. As the nets get wetter, the water trickles down to a trough or pipe. Some nets gather as much as 550 liters (150 gallons) in a day. People use the water from fog nets for drinking, cooking, and farming.

Fog-catching nets do not provide all the water a village needs. But getting water from nets means buying less water from a truck.

Are We on Mars?

Filmmakers are not the only people who visit the Atacama Desert. Scientists also visit this desert. This is because it is similar to Mars in some ways. Like Mars, it has bare, red rock and soil. It has no surface water. Also like Mars, the temperature can change from very, very hot to freezing day to night.

Because of these similarities, the Atacama Desert is useful for testing equipment bound for Mars. Some scientists test-drove a Mars rover there. The rover drilled and tested soil samples using a new method. They tested it in the Atacama to see if it worked before using it on a future Mars mission.

The Atacama is a challenging place to live. But sometimes, the driest place on Earth is exactly where you need to be.

A Mars rover explores the Atacama Desert.

This image of Mars shows how it is similar to the Atacama Desert. So, scientists sometimes test Mars rovers in the desert.

How Is Weather Predicted?

Science Vocabulary

air mass

data

front

meteorologist

Weather affects everyone, everywhere on Earth. Can you predict the weather? Dark clouds may tell you it will rain. But weather is complicated. Scientists measure temperature, wind, and humidity. They look for patterns. These measurements can help predict the weather.

NGSS **3-ESS2-1.** Represent data in tables and graphical displays to describe typical weather conditions expected during a particular season.

ESS2.D. Scientists record patterns of the weather across different times and areas so that they can make predictions about what kind of weather might happen next.

Patterns Patterns of change can be used to make predictions.

Analyzing and Interpreting Data

1. Observing Sky Conditions

Suppose you see dark clouds forming overhead. What do you think the weather will be like? You can often predict weather by observing.

One way to predict weather is by looking at the sky. On a sunny day without clouds, it probably will not rain. By watching clouds move, you can see the direction they are coming from.

Knowing about some types of clouds can help you predict the weather. *Cirrus* clouds are thin, white, and high in the sky. They form in good weather. *Nimbus* clouds are thick, dark clouds that can bring precipitation. *Cumulous* clouds have a low flat base and are white and puffy. They also form in good weather. But if a cumulus cloud grows very tall, it may bring thunderstorms.

This type of tall, flat-topped cumulous cloud could bring rain.

Knowing about clouds can help people predict weather. Short, puffy cumulous clouds like these can form on a sunny day.

2. Describing Air Masses and Fronts

You learned that air is always moving. Knowing how air moves can help predict weather.

Air Masses

Imagine a giant bubble of air floating above several states. If you could move around inside it, you would find that the air temperature is about the same wherever you go. So is the humidity. Air in the atmosphere is like this. A large body of air of the same temperature and humidity is an **air mass**.

An air mass can form over a warm ocean and move onto land. The air mass would bring warm, humid weather with it.

Air masses are described by where they form. Air masses that form over a cold ocean are cold and humid. Air masses that form over a hot desert are hot and dry. Knowing about air masses helps people predict weather. Suppose an air mass forms over a warm ocean and moves over North America. It would bring warm, humid weather with it.

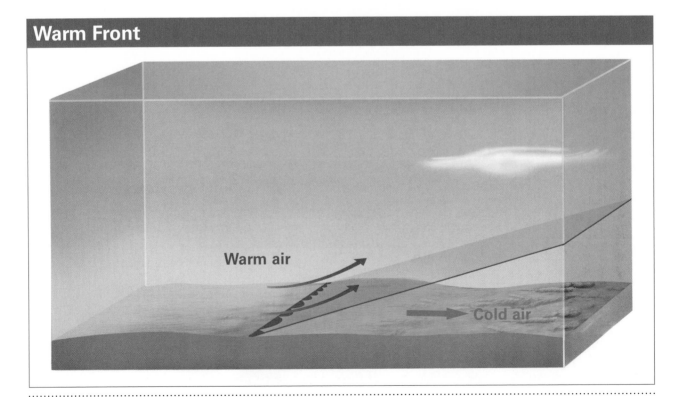

Warm Front

Warm air

Cold air

Fronts

You may have heard someone say, "A front is coming in!" That usually means the weather is about to change.

When one air mass meets another, they do not mix right away. They push against each other. The line where two air masses meet is called a **front**. Fronts often bring weather changes. They are shown on weather maps as blue or red lines. Knowing about fronts can help people predict weather.

For example, a *cold front* is the edge of a cold air mass that is moving into a mass of warmer air. When a cold front meets a warm air mass, cold air moves underneath the warm air. Clouds and thunderstorms can form along the front. As the front passes, the wind changes direction. Once the new air mass is overhead, the skies may clear again. But temperatures are cooler now.

Where two air masses meet, a front forms. Clouds and storms often form along a cold front.

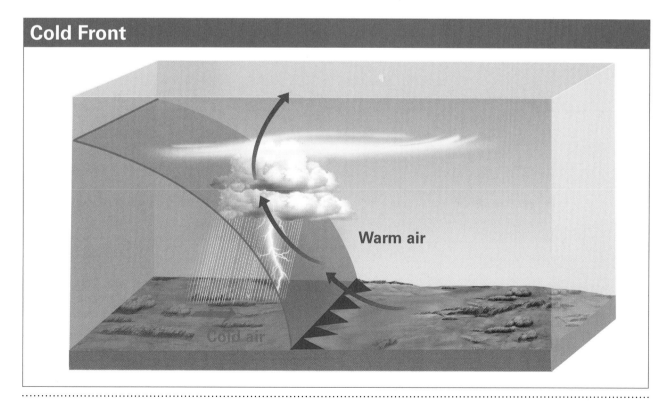

Cold Front

Warm air

Cold air

3. Using Weather Technology

Weather can change from hour to hour. It can change from place to place. Weather is very complicated. To make sense of it, scientists need to do more than observe the sky and weather maps.

Collecting Weather Data

A **meteorologist** is a scientist who studies weather. Meteorologists collect weather data from many different places. **Data** are pieces of information, such as facts or measurements. For example, if you wrote down the temperature, humidity, and wind speed, you would be recording data. Meteorologists collect these kinds of data at all times. But they don't take all the measurements themselves! This is done using weather stations.

Weather stations have tools that observe and record data about weather automatically. They collect data on temperature and precipitation. They collect data on air masses and fronts.

Some weather stations are very simple. In remote places, they report weather data even when people are not there.

Weather stations can be found all over the world. This station at the South Pole collects many kinds of weather data.

Weather Station Locations

Thousands of weather stations are set up all over the world. There are stations on land and on ships at sea. People use computers to understand the data from weather stations to predict the weather.

Weather is not just about the air near the ground. It is also about the air high up in the sky. So, meteorologists launch *weather balloons*. Weather balloons collect data about the air well above Earth's surface. Tools on the balloon collect data about winds and temperature. They send the data to weather stations.

People launch some stations even higher, up into space. These are called *weather satellites*. Weather satellites have tools that collect data about the atmosphere below them. The data are sent to computers on Earth. Scientists use all of this information to track and predict the weather.

It is hard for people to get to the upper atmosphere. So, they launch weather balloons to take measurements there.

Weather satellites in outer space send pictures and weather data back to Earth for people to use.

4. Using Patterns to Predict Weather

Each night the sun sets. Each morning it rises. This is a pattern. There are patterns in weather, too.

Meteorologists study weather patterns to predict weather. Some patterns happen from day to day. It may be sunny every day for a week. Some patterns happen over a season. In parts of Florida, it rains almost every day between May and October.

Patterns can be seen with air masses and fronts. A cold front usually brings storms and a drop in temperature. A warm front can also bring rain. But after the warm front goes through an area the temperature is warmer.

Meteorologists study weather data to make weather maps. This helps them predict what the weather will be like next.

Scientists collect weather data from all over the world. The data are put into computers. They are used to make weather maps, graphs, and charts. Meteorologists also use weather data to make predictions, called forecasts.

Weather Map

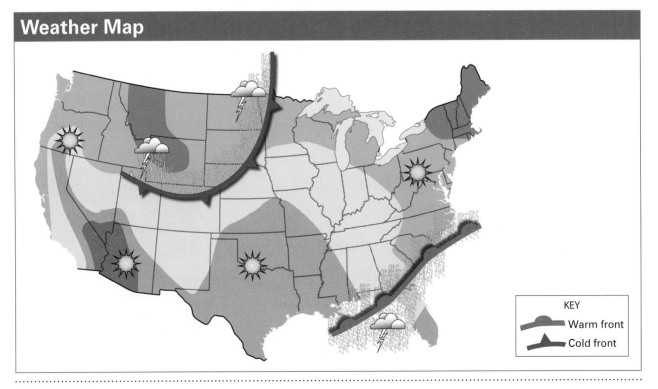

KEY
Warm front
Cold front

How Is Weather Predicted?

1. Observing Sky Conditions   Observing the sky is a simple way to predict weather. Precipitation never falls out of a cloudless sky. Some kinds of clouds form in sunny weather. Other kinds of clouds often bring precipitation.

2. Describing Air Masses and Fronts   Air in the atmosphere moves around in large masses. The line where two air masses meet is called a front. Fronts move over Earth's surface. They bring weather changes, like storms and a drop in temperature.

3. Using Weather Technology   Meteorologists are people who study weather. They use tools to gather data, or pieces of information. The tools are located at weather stations. There are weather stations all over the world. Some are high in the sky or even up in outer space.

4. Using Patterns to Predict Weather   If you study weather, you will see patterns everywhere. Some of these patterns have to do with air masses and fronts. Scientists make and study weather maps to find patterns. They use these patterns to help forecast the weather.

Animal Weather Forecasters

Weather forecasts that use science started less than 150 years ago. Before then, people looked for clues in the sky and in the way animals behaved. Can you really predict the weather by watching animals?

One by one, the cows lay down. The farmer looked up at the cloudy sky. She knew the saying: when cows lay down in the pasture, it was going to rain. Just then, a barn cat sneezed—another sign of rain.

Long ago, old stories and sayings were the only things people had to predict the weather. They looked for changes in animals, plants, and other parts of nature. Today, many people wonder if there is any truth in the old weather sayings. Can these old sayings stand the test of today's science?

People once used animal behaviors to predict the weather. For example, one saying claimed that if cows lie down, rain is on the way.

Groundhog Day

Another animal some people think predicts weather is the groundhog. The old story says that on Groundhog Day, the groundhog takes a break from its winter sleep. It comes out of its den to look around. If it sees its shadow, then there will be six more weeks of winter. If it does not, then an early spring is coming.

In Pennsylvania, thousands gather each Groundhog Day to celebrate. Of course, a wild animal will not come out with all those people watching. Instead, there is a staged show. Men in costumes pretend to listen to a tame groundhog.

This is a lot of fun, but is it accurate? No. Scientists found that there was no pattern to the groundhog's predictions and the arrival of warm weather. In fact, the groundhog was wrong more often than it was right!

Scientists compared Groundhog Day forecasts to actual spring temperatures. The groundhog's forecasts are not often accurate.

The length of a woolly worm's brown band is supposed to predict the coming winter. It does not—but it might say something about last winter's weather.

Woolly Worm Winters

Another weather forecaster is the woolly worm, also called the woolly bear caterpillar. Some say the size of its brown band predicts winter weather. When caterpillars have long brown bands, winter will be warm that year. Short brown bands predict a cold winter.

Many years ago, Dr. Howard Curran, an insect scientist, tested out the saying. He drove into the mountains every fall for eight years. He measured as many woolly worms as he could find. The first three years, the woolly worm saying worked. The next few years it did not.

Later, another scientist made a discovery. If woolly worms hatch in early spring, they have long brown bands the following fall. If they hatch in late spring, they have short bands. So, the bands may say something about last winter, but not next winter.

Sharks Swim to Safety

An animal that may truly predict the weather is the shark. And what we know about shark forecasting does not come from an old weather legend. It is from a recent discovery.

A team of scientists were tracking young sharks. The young sharks lived in shallow water. But, when a hurricane was coming, the sharks did something odd. They swam to deeper water.

Swimming to deeper water made sense. There, the small sharks would be safe from storm waves. But how did the sharks know that a hurricane was coming? Scientists are not sure, but it could be that they sensed changes in the air pressing down on the ocean surface.

Sharks won't be used as weather forecasters. They are too hard to see in the ocean water. But someday you might discover a true weather predicting animal that is easier to track.

Scientists discovered that young sharks swim to deeper water right before a hurricane comes. Doing so protects them from storm waves.

How Are Weather and Climate Related?

Science Vocabulary

climate

desert

equator

Have you noticed patterns in the weather where you live? During certain times of the year, it may rain a lot. The weather may be cool and windy, or it may be hot and dry. The patterns of weather may repeat year after year. This is climate.

NGSS 3-ESS2-2. Obtain and combine information to describe climates in different regions of the world.

ESS2.D. Climate describes a range of an area's typical weather conditions and the extent to which those conditions vary over years.

Patterns Patterns of change can be used to make predictions.

Obtaining, Evaluating, and Communicating Information

1. Where Climate Data Come From

Suppose you are planning a trip to Florida. Would you pack mittens and boots? Knowing Florida's *climate* may help you decide.

It is warm in Florida for many months, year after year. That is its climate. **Climate** is an area's expected weather over a long period of time. Climate is not the same as weather. Florida may have some days with cold weather each year. But Florida's climate is warm. A **desert** is an area with a dry climate. It does not rain much in deserts. In a hot desert, it is hot and dry most of the year. Other deserts are cold.

Climate describes the typical temperature and precipitation over a period of time. Scientists figure out the climate for an area by looking at weather data collected over many years. All of these pieces of information together are called climate data.

Different places on Earth have different climates. They tend to have certain temperatures and certain amounts of rainfall.

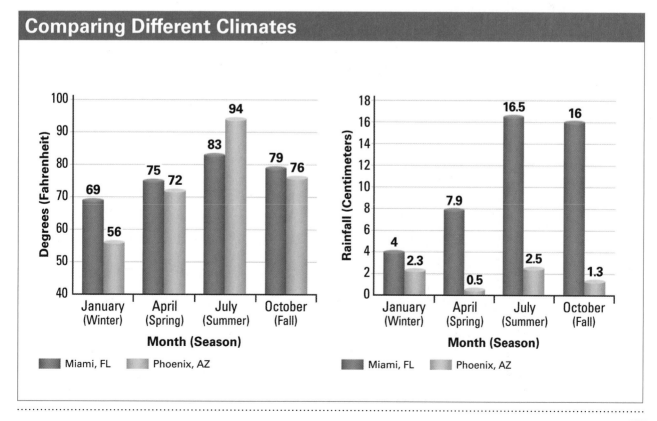

Comparing Different Climates

Left chart: Degrees (Fahrenheit) vs Month (Season)
- January (Winter): Miami, FL 69; Phoenix, AZ 56
- April (Spring): Miami, FL 75; Phoenix, AZ 72
- July (Summer): Miami, FL 83; Phoenix, AZ 94
- October (Fall): Miami, FL 79; Phoenix, AZ 76

Right chart: Rainfall (Centimeters) vs Month (Season)
- January (Winter): Miami, FL 4; Phoenix, AZ 2.3
- April (Spring): Miami, FL 7.9; Phoenix, AZ 0.5
- July (Summer): Miami, FL 16.5; Phoenix, AZ 2.5
- October (Fall): Miami, FL 16; Phoenix, AZ 1.3

■ Miami, FL   ■ Phoenix, AZ

2. Climates Around the World

Places near the *equator* get a lot of sunlight and have warm climates. The **equator** is an imaginary line around Earth. It is midway between the North and South Poles. Places farther away from the equator have cooler climates. The climate is coldest at the North and South Poles. There are different climates all around the world.

Tropical Climates

Places near the equator have *tropical climates*. Tropical climates are hot. They have high temperatures that do not change much all year long. Many tropical climates are rainy. A tropical rainforest is rainy for much of the year. There can be thunderstorms almost every day. Other tropical climates are drier. A *savanna* is warm all year long and most have a long dry season. Not as many trees grow in a savanna compared to a tropical rainforest.

Tropical rainforests have hot, wet climates that allow for a lot of tree growth. Savannas are warm, too, but their drier climate leads to more open, grassy areas.

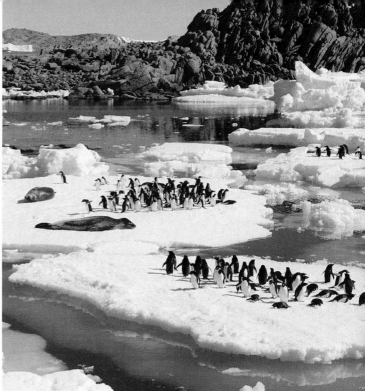

Temperate Climates

Places farther away from the equator to the north and south have different climates. Most of the United States and southern Canada have *temperate climates*. So do some places in the Southern Hemisphere like New Zealand. Temperate climates have both warm and cold temperatures. They usually have four seasons. The summers in temperate climates are warm or hot. The winters are cool or cold.

Polar Climates

Places farthest away from the equator have *polar climates*. Polar climates are very cold. The North and South poles have polar climates. So do the far northern parts of Canada and Alaska. The land and water are covered with snow or ice for most of the year. At the South Pole in Antarctica, the temperature is below freezing all the time. Antarctica's climate is cold and dry.

Temperate climates usually have four seasons. Polar climates are very cold, and finding food on land is difficult.

Climate data can be used to design buildings. Engineers might choose to build homes in hot, dry places with adobe because it keeps homes cool.

3. Using Climate Data

You have probably eaten corn during summer. What kind of climate is best for growing corn?

Climate data can be helpful to people. Farmers use climate data to decide what crops to plant. Farmers study the temperature and rainfall patterns. Some crops need cool temperatures or dry soil. Corn needs plenty of sunshine and a lot of water to grow well. In the United States, much corn is grown in the Midwest. Orange trees need warm climates. They are grown in Florida and California. Farmers also use climate data to decide the best time to plant seeds or harvest crops.

Engineers use climate data to design buildings. Adobe is a material that keeps homes cool in warm temperatures. Adobe brick is used often in hot, dry climates. Engineers would choose other materials for buildings in cold and wet climates.

How Are Weather and Climate Related?

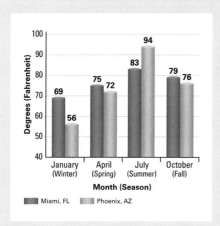

1. Where Climate Data Come From Climate is an area's typical weather over many years. Some areas have climates that are cold or warm. Climates can also be dry or wet. Scientists learn about climates. They look at an area's weather data collected over many years. All of this information and the patterns within it are climate data.

2. Climates Around the World One of the biggest effects on climate is how much sunlight an area gets. Areas near the equator get a lot of sunlight. They have tropical climates like rainforests and savannas. Areas near the poles get much less sun. They have cold, icy climates. Temperate climates are found in between these two. Much of the United States is temperate. Temperate climates have four seasons.

3. Using Climate Data Knowing about climate can be very helpful to people. Farmers need to understand their climate. This lets them plant the right crops at the right times. Some engineers design buildings. They can use their knowledge of an area's climate. Some materials and designs work better in certain climates than others.

Wild Turkeys Are Back

Forests and animals grow in New England's wet temperate climate. But the first English settlers there cut the forest down, and the animals disappeared. What made them disappear?

In 1621, the English colonists at Plymouth welcomed their Native American neighbors to join their feast of Thanksgiving. Did they eat wild turkeys? It is likely. At the time, plenty of turkeys lived in the thick forests around Plymouth.

In 1863, President Lincoln announced the first national Thanksgiving Day. But by then, there were no wild turkeys left in New England. What happened to the fall holiday's favorite bird?

New England had plenty of wild turkeys in 1621. But they had disappeared by 1863.

Wild turkeys need forest trees to survive. But settlers had destroyed much of the forest that wild turkeys lived in.

Wild Turkeys Out, Tame Turkeys In

Wild turkeys disappeared because they had nowhere left to live. Wild turkeys live in forests with a few open spaces. They use the trees in a forest to hide from predators. They also sleep in trees. Wild turkeys survive by eating food in forests. They eat plants, insects, fruits, and nuts that fall from trees.

By 1863, farmers had cut down more than two-thirds of the forests in New England. They planted crops in their place. They also used the land as pasture. They used the trees as timber for building homes. Chickens, geese, and barnyard turkeys scratched the ground where wild turkeys used to peck at the forest floor.

Trees now surround a stone wall that once marked the edge of an open pasture.

In New England, fields that are not farmed will turn back into forests.

Abandoned Farms and Fields

The open land needed for farming is not usual for the area. New England has a wet temperate climate. Rain or snow falls in every month of the year there. This is the kind of climate that grows trees. Forests need a lot of water to grow. So, trees grow very well in New England. Unless farmers keep farming, the land on a farm will grow other plants again. The plants that grow will not be the same as those usually grown on a farm.

Between the 1860s and the 1940s, many farmers stopped farming. Some moved west to find better land. Others took jobs in factories. Wildflowers and grasses began to grow in unplowed fields. Then shrubs took hold among the grasses. Finally, tall trees soared again over forest floors that were once sunny pastures.

Wild Turkeys Return

Thanks to New England's climate, the land was turkey-friendly again. Even so, the turkeys did not return right away. They lived too far away to get there on their own.

So, in the 1970s, people caught turkeys in places where they still lived, such as Pennsylvania. Then they moved them to New England. Their efforts paid off! Today, turkeys are in many places. You can hear gobbling sounds at birdfeeders. You can see large flocks crossing the road. Some even come up to cars and peck at the windows.

The forest that grew well in the climate came back. But climate might not bring back every environment that people have changed. Cutting down trees can change landscapes forever. But, in one place at least, the forests—and the turkeys—have returned.

The forests that grow well in New England's climate returned. Then people helped bring back the turkeys.

How Does Extreme Weather Affect People?

Science Vocabulary

blizzard

dust storm

hurricane

thunderstorm

tornado

wildfire

Rainy weather brings water needed by plants and animals to survive. Snow may be fun for you to play in. But weather can be so strong it causes damage. Tornadoes, blizzards, and hurricanes are examples of extreme weather. You cannot prevent severe weather. But you can take steps to reduce its harm and stay safe.

NGSS **3-ESS3-1.** Make a claim about the merit of a design solution that reduces the impacts of a weather-related hazard.

ESS3.B. A variety of natural hazards result from natural processes. Humans cannot eliminate natural hazards but can take steps to reduce their impacts.

Cause and Effect Cause and effect relationships are routinely identified, tested, and used to explain change.

 **Engaging in Argument from Evidence**

1. Extreme Weather

Clear, sunny days can be nice. But some weather is not so pleasant.

Temperature, wind, and precipitation can come together and create powerful storms. In 2012 a storm known as Superstorm Sandy moved up the East Coast of the United States. The storm was so big, it measured more than 1450 km (900 mi) across. Along the coast, the rain and ocean waves caused flooding. Farther west in some places, up to 1 m (3 ft) of snow fell. The storm caused a lot of damage and people died.

Some storms have very strong winds and heavy, pounding rain. Other storms have cold temperatures and blowing snow. What kinds of storms happen where you live? You can make a plan to prepare for a storm and stay safe. Talk with your family so you know what to do if a storm comes.

Rain and ocean waves caused flooding during Superstorm Sandy.

Superstorm Sandy caused wind and flood damage. City streets filled with ocean water, sand, and mud.

Lightning Strikes per Year in Different Cities	
Tampa, FL	100
New Orleans, LA	60
Detroit, MI	30
Boston, MA	20
San Francisco, CA	5

Thunderstorms are much more common in some areas than others. In general, there are more thunderstorms closer to the equator.

2. Thunderstorms

Dark clouds can bring rain. Only some produce thunderstorms. During these storms, you may hear the loud clap of thunder or see flashes of lightning.

A **thunderstorm** is a strong storm that brings wind, rain, thunder, and lightning. Thunderstorms happen all over the world. Most occur during spring and summer. Florida gets more thunderstorms than other states, but they can happen in any state.

A thunderstorm forms when warm air flows up while cold air flows down. This movement of air creates a tall cloud that produces wind and rain.

The lightning produced by thunderstorms can damage whatever it strikes. It can kill or seriously injure people. What can you do to stay safe during a thunderstorm? If you hear thunder or see lightning, go indoors. If you are not near a building, find a low place or stay in a car. Stay away from tall objects.

Thunderstorms are powerful storms that produce large amounts of rain, winds, and dangerous lightning. If you see a thunderstorm coming your way, go inside a building.

3. Hurricanes

Hurricanes are larger than thunderstorms. A **hurricane** is a large, spinning storm that forms over a tropical ocean. Hurricanes gain strength as they move over warm water. It rains very hard in a hurricane. They have strong winds that can cause ocean waters to rise and cause flooding.

Hurricanes get energy from warm, humid air above the ocean. When a hurricane reaches land or cold waters, it loses its energy and weakens. Most hurricanes form in late summer and early fall.

You can prepare for a hurricane. Put objects away that could be picked up by strong winds. Have flashlights and batteries ready in case you lose electric power. During a hurricane you should stay inside. Some people near the coast are told to go inland. They can stay in shelters until the storm ends.

Hurricanes are large, spinning storms. From above Earth, you can see a hurricane's spiral shape and spinning motion.

A tornado is a short-lived mass of swirling winds that forms in certain types of clouds. Some tornadoes move across the ground and can cause a lot of damage.

4. Tornadoes

Imagine a wind so strong it can turn a car upside down or blow apart a house. What can cause that?

A **tornado** is a powerful, quickly spinning air mass. Many tornadoes form during thunderstorms. Tornadoes are much, much smaller than hurricanes. But their winds move faster. The spinning winds can reach over 480 kilometers per hour (300 miles per hour). More than 1000 tornadoes form each year in the United States. Tornadoes can happen in any state. Most strike in the Great Plains.

Tornadoes form quickly, so there may be little warning or time to prepare. They usually only last for a few minutes. A *tornado warning* means a tornado is headed your way. You should quickly move to a safe place. Go to a basement or a bathroom or closet without windows. If you are at school, follow directions from your teachers.

5. Blizzards

You know that storms can happen in warm weather. Cold-weather storms can happen, too.

A **blizzard** is a long-lasting snowstorm with a lot of falling or blowing snow. Blizzards have low temperatures and gusty winds. The winds cause snowdrifts to form. Blizzards most often occur in the Midwest and Northeast areas of the United States. In 1993, a blizzard formed over a large part of the Southeast. Parts of southern Alabama got 30 cm (1 ft) of snow. Some mountain areas in Tennessee got nearly 1.5 m (5 ft) of snow.

The safest place during a blizzard is indoors. Cold temperatures can cause frostbite. It is hard to see in blowing snow. Roads can be hard to drive or walk on. It is best to wait out the storm indoors. You might even get a snow day!

Blizzards bring cold temperatures, wind, and snowfall. Blowing snow can create large drifts and make driving impossible.

6. Dust Storms and Wildfires

Sometimes weather causes other kinds of storms. Have you ever seen dust swirling in the air?

Some places are hit by *dust storms*. How can a storm be made of dust? Sometimes during droughts, plants do not grow and the soil becomes dry. A **dust storm** forms when dry soil is picked up by strong winds. They form big blowing clouds of dust.

Dust storms form when large amounts of loose soil are picked up by wind. The dust can cause damage when it blows over cities and farms.

Dry weather can cause other hazards, too. Some places get dangerous wildfires. A **wildfire** is a large fire in a forest or grassland. Wildfires can be started by lightning. Other wildfires are started by humans. If the land is dry, the fire will quickly spread. It can burn for days or months. Wind can make wildfires worse because it spreads the flames. Natural fires in areas without people can be helpful. But fires near people's houses can be dangerous. Wildfires burn fast, so people may need to leave quickly for safety.

Lightning can start some wildfires. Other wildfires are started by people.

How Does Extreme Weather Affect People?

1. Extreme Weather   Temperature, wind, and water can come together to create powerful storms. There are different kinds of storms in different climates. People can prepare to stay safer during storms.

2. Thunderstorms   One type of extreme weather is thunderstorms. Thunderstorms bring large amounts of rain, wind, and lightning. All of these can be dangerous. You should stay indoors during a thunderstorm to stay safe.

3. Hurricanes   Hurricanes are large, spinning storms that form over tropical oceans. They are much larger than thunderstorms. When they hit land, hurricanes can cause flooding. The strong winds cause damage.

4. Tornadoes   Tornadoes are powerful, quickly spinning masses of air. They are much, much smaller than hurricanes, but their winds can be faster. Tornadoes often come from thunderstorms. They are very dangerous.

5. Blizzards   Blizzards are very powerful snowstorms. They are cold and usually drop large amounts of snow. Strong winds can make it hard to see, so driving is dangerous. It is best to stay warm indoors during a blizzard.

6. Dust Storms and Wildfires   Sometimes it does not rain much. Dust storms come from strong winds during dry conditions. Dry conditions can also lead to wildfires. Some wildfires are good, but fires near people are dangerous.

Weather Beacons

You might search the Web to learn what the weather is like where you live. But how did people get weather forecasts before television or the Internet?

It is 1953 in Boston, Massachusetts. A boy and his father are walking to a baseball game, but the weather is cloudy. In Boston, the weather can change quickly. "Look at the Hancock," his dad says. The boy sees the tower flashing blue! The game is still on!

It was not always easy to get a weather forecast back then. Newspaper forecasts were often wrong by the time they were printed. Televisions were uncommon, radios were not always handy, and the Internet was not around yet. So, many big cities had a weather beacon, which is a light on top of a tall building. The color of the light showed the weather forecast.

Many big cities had a weather beacon on top of a tall building to tell people the weather.

Some cities still have weather beacons. The flashing colors are like a secret code that tells the weather forecast. A poem explains the colors in the Boston beacon:

> Steady blue, clear view.
> Flashing blue, clouds due.
> Steady red, rain ahead.
> Flashing red, snow instead.

The Boston weather beacon gets updated when someone calls a weather service for the forecast. Other, newer weather beacons have computerized instruments to check the current weather and update the display. Even though you can now look up the weather online, it's fun to get weather reports by secret code!

The different colors of the Boston weather beacon represent different types of weather.

John Hancock Weather Beacon

How Can People Reduce Extreme Weather Damage?

Science Vocabulary

lightning rod

Extreme weather can be very dangerous. As you have learned, Earth's atmosphere is always changing and moving. Events like tornadoes, thunderstorms, and hurricanes will continue to happen. People can do things to protect themselves and others.

NGSS | **3-ESS3-1.** Make a claim about the merit of a design solution that reduces the impacts of a weather-related hazard. | **ESS3.B.** A variety of natural hazards result from natural processes. Humans cannot eliminate natural hazards but can take steps to reduce their impacts. | **Cause and Effect** Cause and effect relationships are routinely identified, tested, and used to explain change. |  **Engaging in Argument from Evidence**

1. Scientists Investigate Storms

You have learned about many kinds of storms. Some are dangerous. Storms won't stop coming. But people can learn more about them.

Scientists study storms to help keep people safe. For example, scientists study tornadoes. They use radar. They observe thunderstorm clouds. Scientists study wind speed and direction. By studying weather, scientists have found patterns. There are certain wind patterns that tend to form tornadoes.

In the spring of 2013, meteorologists predicted a tornado would hit near Oklahoma City. They put out a warning. People had 16 minutes to get to safety. Warnings like these save people's lives. Scientists keep studying tornadoes. They hope to find ways to warn people sooner.

Scientists have studied the patterns of when and where tornadoes have occurred. They are learning to predict when tornadoes are about to form.

Tornado Risk Map

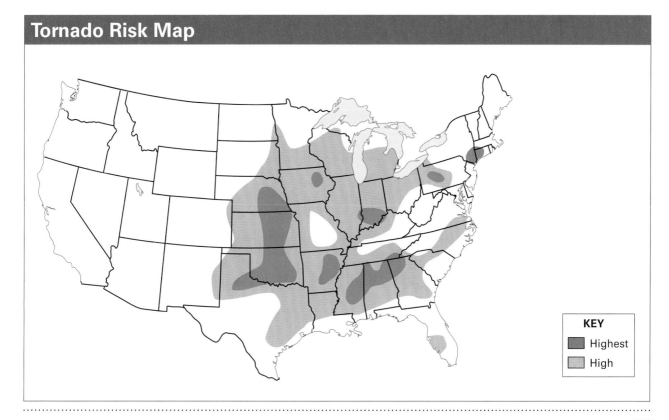

KEY

Highest

High

⚙ *Engineering Design*

2. Engineers Help Reduce Storm Damage

You have learned about thunderstorms. You know that lightning strikes can damage trees, buildings, and other objects. Lightning usually strikes the tallest or highest object in an area.

Lightning Rods

Engineers design new things and improve old ones. Some engineers design *lightning rods*. **Lightning rods** are structures that protect objects from lightning. A lightning rod is always taller than the objects around it. That way, lightning will strike the rod and not the other objects.

Lightning rods can protect a home or other buildings. Lightning moves down the rod to the ground and does not go through the building.

A lightning rod can protect a house. The metal lightning rod stands up on the top of a roof. The rod is connected to a wire that goes into the ground. When lightning strikes the rod, electricity moves safely to the ground through the wire. Electricity moves through the rod and wire instead of going through the house.

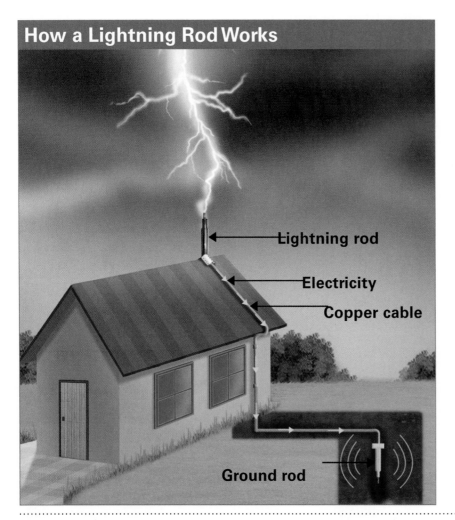

How a Lightning Rod Works

Lightning rod

Electricity

Copper cable

Ground rod

Engineers build artificial lightning machines to create electricity and test their designs.

Testing Lightning Rods

Engineers design different kinds of lightning rods. For large buildings, engineers might use many rods together with wires connecting them. When lightning strikes anywhere on the building, it moves along the rods and wires to the ground.

Engineers make models of their designs. The model rod and buildings are smaller than the real ones. But they are made of the same materials and are in the same shapes.

The engineers test their models to see if they work. Where do they get the lightning? Engineers build artificial lightning machines to create the electricity. This can be dangerous, but engineers know how to do it safely. They test the model to find out if the rod works as it should. If electricity is not carried to the ground safely, then the design failed. New materials or a new design are needed.

Engineers use lightning machines to test how well their design and materials work. Here, they are testing a lightning rod.

3. Communities Help Reduce Storm Danger

Suppose a hurricane is predicted to hit your town. What are some ways you can stay safe?

Hurricanes and other storms can affect many people. But people in a community can work together. They can plan ways to keep safe during storms. Some communities set up shelters at schools, hotels, or other places. Shelters are safe places to stay during a storm. Shelters store food and water. They have a place for people to sleep. People stay in shelters until the storm is over.

Sometimes it is unsafe to return home right after a storm. In 2005, when Hurricane Katrina hit New Orleans, Louisiana, many residents had to leave their homes. Because the flooding was so bad, many could not go home right away. Some had to stay in shelters for months. Extreme weather is dangerous, but people can help each other through the problems.

When a storm hits, many communities set up shelters for people whose homes are no longer safe. The shelters are often set up in large buildings like schools.

How Can People Reduce Extreme Weather Damage?

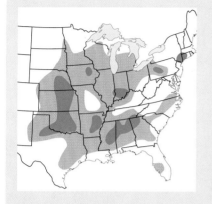

1. Scientists Investigate Storms Extreme weather is a part of life. It cannot be stopped. But people can prepare for weather hazards if they know it is coming. Scientists study storms to keep people safe. Studying patterns in weather can help predict hazards like tornadoes. Scientists issue warnings to help save people's lives.

2. Engineers Help Reduce Storm Damage Lightning is dangerous to people and buildings. Engineers design solutions to help keep them safe. Lightning rods are placed above buildings. This way lightning strikes the rod. It transfers the electricity safely to the ground. Engineers are always testing their designs to make them better.

3. Communities Help Reduce Storm Danger
Scientists try to warn communities that extreme weather is coming. Then people in communities can work together to help keep everyone safe. Some communities set up shelters in places like schools. People can go to the shelter to stay safe until the storm is over.

Weather on Fire

Weather can start wildfires. It can also determine how far they spread. How do meteorologists help with wildfires?

Weather conditions can make a wildfire burn for a long time and spread quickly.

It was August 2012. Summer heat had been baking northern California for weeks. Grass and shrubs were dry. Then lightning struck, and fire raced across the landscape. Crews of firefighters arrived, set up camp, and got to work. They had been fighting fires for three months already, but they would work their hardest to contain this new blaze.

The Rush Fire started in northeast California and spread to Nevada. Three weeks later, it was over. But it was the second-largest wildfire in California history. Weather conditions before and during the fire made it burn and spread as quickly and as far as it did.

Signs tell people when to be extra careful.

The climate in some western states, like California, is especially fire-prone. Spring gets rain, but the rest of the year is dry. Plants grow quickly in the wet spring. Then the hot summer weather dries them out. The dry plants become fuel for a wildfire. All it takes is a campfire or sparks from power lines to start a fire.

But weather affects fire risk more than anything else. Lightning strikes are one way that weather causes fires. For this reason, the National Weather Service does fire weather forecasts. Have you seen signs about fire risk along the road? The level of risk stated on the sign comes from a fire weather report. The signs let people know when it is not safe to have campfires or to use power tools.

Wildfires are most common in places that have hot, dry summers. The heat dries up the grass and trees.

Blazing Hot Winds

Once a wildfire starts, the weather plays a big part in what happens next. Wind causes a fire to spread quickly. And fire even creates its own wind! Hot air from the flames rises and cools. So, it rushes back along the ground and makes the fire spread.

Wind from a fire is tricky. It may suddenly shift direction, taking the fire with it. The fire crew can end up in the wrong place. Weather forecasts help firefighters that fight wildfires. So, special wildfire meteorologists set up weather stations at the biggest fires. They are called *incident meteorologists*. They keep track of the weather in the area and of the wind from the fire. The fire chief counts on these meteorologists for forecasts that are specifically made for that fire.

Some meteorologists help forecast weather at wildfires.

Fighting the Fire

When it comes to fighting wildfires, weather is just part of the picture. A fire chief also needs to know what kind of fuel is in the fire's path. There could be trees or dry grass in its path. The locations of nearby towns are also important.

This information helps the fire chief choose the best ways to stop that fire. Crews may need to cut down trees. Or they might use helicopters to drop water on the fire. The fire chief must come up with solutions quickly. If one way does not work, it's time to try another.

When a wildfire is over, the crews work on fire prevention. They cut brush and clear land. But weather is unpreventable! So, even with these measures, fire crews must be prepared to fight the next wildfire.

Dry grass is fuel for wildfires. Fire crews work hard to put out and then prevent wildfires.

Life Cycles and Traits

It is a sunny day at the park. There, you spot a mother duck and her ducklings waddling by. You observe that, in some ways, the ducklings are like their parent. They all have orange beaks and feet. In other ways, they are not like their mother. The ducklings have fuzzy yellow feathers. The mother has smooth white feathers. In this unit, you will discover why plants and animals can be similar to and different from their parents.

216

Unit Contents

Unit 4 Overview

Graphic Organizer: This unit is structured to introduce **traits**, highlight the **consequences** of a variation of traits, and compare the traits of organisms with different **life cycles**.

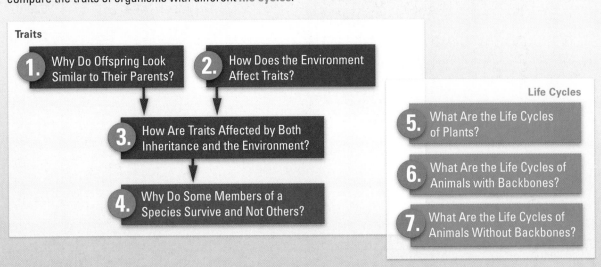

Traits

1. Why Do Offspring Look Similar to Their Parents?

2. How Does the Environment Affect Traits?

3. How Are Traits Affected by Both Inheritance and the Environment?

4. Why Do Some Members of a Species Survive and Not Others?

Life Cycles

5. What Are the Life Cycles of Plants?

6. What Are the Life Cycles of Animals with Backbones?

7. What Are the Life Cycles of Animals Without Backbones?

NGSS Next Generation Science Standards

Performance Expectations

3-LS1-1. Develop models to describe that organisms have unique and diverse life cycles but all have in common birth, growth, reproduction, and death.

3-LS3-1. Analyze and interpret data to provide evidence that plants and animals have traits inherited from parents and that variation of these traits exists in a group of similar organisms.

3-LS3-2. Use evidence to support the explanation that traits can be influenced by the environment.

3-LS4-2. Use evidence to construct an explanation for how the variations in characteristics among individuals of the same species may provide advantages in surviving, finding mates, and reproducing.

Disciplinary Core Ideas

LS1.B: Growth and Development of Organisms

• Reproduction is essential to the continued existence of every kind of organism. Plants and animals have unique and diverse life cycles.

LS3.A: Inheritance of Traits

• Many characteristics of organisms are inherited from their parents.

• Other characteristics result from individuals' interactions with the environment, which can range from diet to learning. Many characteristics involve both inheritance and environment.

LS3.B: Variation of Traits

• Different organisms vary in how they look and function because they have different inherited information.

• The environment also affects the traits that an organism develops.

LS4.B: Natural Selection

• Sometimes the differences in characteristics between individuals of the same species provide advantages in surviving, finding mates, and reproducing.

Crosscutting Concepts

Patterns

• Similarities and differences in patterns can be used to sort and classify natural phenomena.

• Patterns of change can be used to make predictions.

Cause and Effect

• Cause and effect relationships are routinely identified and used to explain change.

 Developing and Using Models

 Analyzing and Interpreting Data

 Constructing Explanations and Designing Solutions

Have you ever wondered...

If you compare a baby animal to its parents, you can observe how an animal changes as it grows. This unit will help you answer these questions and many others you may ask.

Why do baby animals look different from their parents?

How does a caterpillar turn into a butterfly?

Why do roses have prickles?

Why Do Offspring Look Similar to Their Parents?

Science Vocabulary

inherited trait

offspring

species

trait

What similarities do you notice between this cat and her kittens? Living things of the same kind have similar traits, or characteristics. Some traits are passed from a parent to its young. But other traits are not. You will discover how these traits can make living things of the same kind look different.

3-LS3-1. Analyze and interpret data to provide evidence that plants and animals have traits inherited from parents and that variation of these traits exists in a group of similar organisms.

LS3.A. Many characteristics of organisms are inherited from their parents.
LS3.B. Different organisms vary in how they look and function because they have different inherited information.

Patterns • Similarities and differences in patterns can be used to sort and classify natural phenomena. • Patterns of change can be used to make predictions.

Analyzing and Interpreting Data

1. Different Animal and Plant Species Exist

You know that goldfish and lions are different. They look and act differently. That is because goldfish and lions are different *species*.

A **species** is a group of living things of the same kind. Members of an animal species produce young of the same species. For example, there are many different crab species. Coconut crabs and flower crabs are different crab species. Each crab species produces young of the same species. Coconut crabs produce young coconut crabs. Flower crabs produce young flower crabs.

Members of a plant species also produce young of the same species. There are many different maple tree species. For example, sugar maple, silver maple, and bigleaf maple are different maple tree species. Each maple tree species produces young of the same species.

These crabs are all different species. There are many different species of crab, and they all produce young of their same species.

Coconut crab

Flower crab

Japanese spider crab

2. Species Have Traits and Produce Offspring

What is a goat like? What about a fish? Do fish and goats look and act the same? Goats have fur and eat grass. Fish have fins and swim in water. They have different *traits*.

Traits are characteristics that living things have. Different species have different traits. For example, different bird species have feathers with different color patterns. Northern Cardinals have many red feathers. Blue Jays have blue, white, and black feathers. Brown Pelicans have gray, white, and brown feathers.

All species also make more members of their own species called **offspring**. For example, baby white-tailed deer are offspring of adult white-tailed deer. You are offspring of adult humans. Plants also produce offspring. For example, young sugar maple trees are offspring of adult sugar maple trees.

Feather color is a trait. The Northern Cardinal on the left will have offspring with red feathers. The Blue Jay's offspring will have its blue, white, and black feathers.

3. Animals and Plants Pass on Traits

At a petting zoo, you may have seen baby goats and their mothers. In what ways do baby goats look like their mothers? What color is their fur?

A characteristic passed by a parent to its offspring is an **inherited trait**. Fur color in goats is an inherited trait. Beak shape and feather color in birds are inherited traits. Different species look different because they have different inherited traits.

Plants also pass on inherited traits to their offspring. A pine tree has needle-shaped leaves. Offspring of that pine tree will have similar leaves. Having needle-shaped leaves is an inherited trait.

Another common inherited trait in plants is how tall a plant can grow. A hollyhock plant can grow to be over 6 m (almost 20 ft). Offspring of that hollyhock plant can also grow to be that tall.

This goat kid inherited some of its traits from its parents. Fur color is an inherited trait.

Many human traits are inherited. For example, this child has inherited her eye color from her mother.

4. Offspring Are Similar to Their Parents

Think of a mother duck and her ducklings. What similar traits do you think they might share?

A mother duck may look a bit different from her ducklings. But most of the ducklings' traits are similar to their parents. When the ducklings become adults, they will be even more similar to their parents. The mother duck and her ducklings all have two legs and webbed feet. They all walk and swim the same way.

Organisms *inherit*, or receive, traits from their parents. An organism is any living thing, like a dog or a tulip. Most humans inherit traits such as having two legs and being able to walk. Humans have a mixture of traits from both of their parents. They may have inherited their mother's hair color and nose shape. They may have also inherited their father's eye color and mouth shape.

Other animals also inherit traits from their parents. A bat inherits its fur color and ability to fly. It also inherits ears that can hear high-pitched sounds. A goldfish inherits its scale color and fin shape from its parents. It also inherits gills it uses to breathe in water. Spiders that spin webs produce offspring that spin webs. Spiders that hunt for food on the ground produce offspring that do the same. A dog may inherit its mother's coat color but get the length of its fur from its father.

Plants also inherit traits from their parents. An oak tree inherits its branching pattern and basic leaf shape from its parents. It will also produce acorns, like its parents do.

Animals inherit traits from their parents. This spider's offspring will also spin webs like their parent does.

5. Offspring Can Be Different from Their Parents

You have learned that puppies in a group often do not look exactly like one another. Some may have different fur colors. One may be black, while two are brown, and another is spotted.

Animals of a species can have traits that are not the same as their parents. A goat has hooves and fur like its parents. But it may have horns that are a different length from its parents. It may also have a broken horn, unlike its parents. Some traits are inherited from parents. Some are not.

Plants of a species can also have traits that are not the same as their parents. Healthy common daisy plants have stems, leaves, and white petals. But some common daisy offspring may have stems that are taller than their parents'. Some may have petals that are thinner or wider. Stem height and petal width are traits that can be different between offspring and their parents.

Even though offspring inherit many traits from their parents, they do not look exactly like one another. These puppies look slightly different from their parents and from each other.

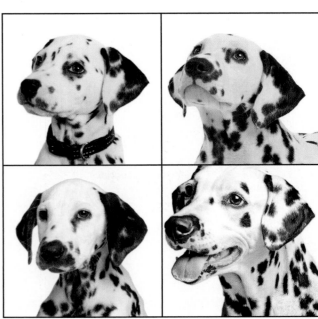

Why Do Offspring Look Similar to Their Parents?

1. Different Animal and Plant Species Exist   There are many different species, or kinds, of plants and animals. Organisms of different species usually look and act differently. Members of a species produce young of the same species.

2. Species Have Traits and Produce Offspring   All animals and plants can produce more of their same species. Their young are called offspring. All living things have traits. Traits are characteristics like having fur, or being able to fly.

3. Animals and Plants Pass on Traits   Plants and animals pass inherited traits to their offspring. For example, animals with fur usually pass fur color on to their offspring. Plants pass the kinds of leaves they make on to their offspring.

4. Offspring Are Similar to Their Parents   Offspring that inherit traits from their parents look similar. Baby animals may inherit fur color, eye color, and body shape. Plant offspring may inherit leaf shape, fruit size, and stem height.

5. Offspring Can Be Different from Their Parents   Not all traits are inherited. Animal and plant offspring usually do not look identical to their parents because some of their traits are not inherited.

The Cutest Baby Face

Baby animals have many of the same traits that their parents have. But most people would agree that babies of many species are cuter than adults. What makes a baby animal cute?

Wrinkled lips, rough skin, and big ears—a rhinoceros may not sound very cute. But baby rhinos sure are. Why? First, let's look at the differences between adult and baby animals.

Baby animals are much smaller than their parents. But size is not the only way you know they are babies. Sometimes baby animals do not have all of the same parts that an adult has. Baby animals also move differently than adults. They might wobble more when they walk.

Many of these differences are similar from one kind of animal to the next. That is why it's usually easy to tell that an animal is a baby, even if you don't know what species it is!

A baby rhinoceros is much smaller than its mother and does not have a horn. These are some of the reasons it is cute.

Signs of Cuteness—Large Head and Eyes

Every species of baby animal is cute in its own special way. But most animal babies share some obvious signs of cuteness.

One sign is that babies have large heads. A baby's head may be smaller than an adult's head. But it is large for its body size. A human baby's head is about one quarter of its whole height. But an adult human can have a head that is only about one-seventh of its height. The baby's head makes up much more of its body.

Another sign of cuteness is large eyes. Most baby animals have eyes that are large for their faces. That's because eyes do not grow as much as other body parts do as the baby grows up. So, the eyes are almost full-sized when the baby is born. Compared with the rest of the baby's face, its eyes appear very large.

Baby animals often have big eyes and a big head, like this lion cub.

One feature that makes baby animals cute is having a round face. This grey seal pup's face is much rounder than an adult's face.

Sign of Cuteness—Round Face

Other signs of cuteness are also found on a baby's head. The shape of a baby's face and the size of its facial features are some reasons why it is cute.

One sign of cuteness is a round face. Baby faces are much rounder than adult faces. Another sign of cuteness is a baby's small features. Adult animals may have large noses, snouts, or beaks. Their ears may be long and pointy. Even though babies have big eyes, all their other features are much smaller. They have smaller mouths, noses, and ears. Since their features are smaller, their round faces look even rounder. As the baby animals grow up, these features get larger and often pointier.

The Power of Cuteness

Being cute isn't just for fun. It can actually be a matter of life or death! Many animals have babies that cannot find food on their own. They need an adult to feed them and keep them safe. If a baby animal seems cute to its parents, they are more likely to take care of it. So, the baby is more likely to survive and grow up to be an adult.

Scientists have found that people are more likely to think a baby is cute if it has certain features, like big eyes. They showed pictures of the same baby to people. In some pictures, the scientists had changed the baby's eyes to look bigger. In other pictures, they had changed the eyes to look smaller. People who looked at the pictures thought that the one with the baby that had bigger eyes was cuter. That is the power of cuteness!

When a baby seems cute, it encourages the parent to care for it and help it survive.

How Does the Environment Affect Traits?

Science Vocabulary

environment

learned behavior

Why do these plants look dry and brown? You will learn how the environment can cause an organism's traits to change. Plants in dry environments may turn dry and brown. Many animals' traits, including those of humans, are also affected by the environment.

NGSS **3-LS3-2.** Use evidence to support the explanation that traits can be influenced by the environment.

LS3.A. Other characteristics result from individuals' interactions with the environment, which can range from diet to learning. Many characteristics involve both inheritance and environment. **LS3.B.** The environment also affects the traits that an organism develops.

Cause and Effect Cause and effect relationships are routinely identified and used to explain change.

Constructing Explanations and Designing Solutions

1. Some Traits Are Not Passed to Offspring

Have you ever seen a small, stunted plant? It may have grown that way because it did not get enough water. Or maybe it did not get enough sunlight. The environment caused that plant to have those traits.

An organism can gain or lose traits in its lifetime. Some traits are caused by the *environment* and are not passed on from parents. The **environment** is all the living and nonliving things that surround an organism. A tree may have holes and markings on its trunk because woodpeckers drilled into it. The woodpeckers are part of the tree's environment. Flamingoes are birds with pinkish coloring. The chicks are not this color when they hatch. They get their color from the food they eat. The food they eat is part of their environment.

Flamingoes are not brightly colored when they hatch. They get that trait from the food they eat in their environment.

2. Traits Can Change in Animals

Have you ever told a dog to sit or roll over? Dogs are not born knowing how to do this.

The things an animal does are traits. Some of those traits are learned. A **learned behavior** is a trait that an organism learns during its lifetime. Animals can learn new behaviors. Some owls may learn to hunt new types of prey. A wolf that lost a limb may learn to walk on three legs. An animal may eat a plant that tastes bad. It will learn not to eat that plant again. Animals learn from their environments.

Some traits change because of something that happened in the animal's environment. A hamster that is overfed can gain weight. It may not be able to run as fast. A lion that has been in a fight may get scratched or clawed. Its injuries will heal, but its skin may be scarred. These scars are traits.

Some organisms learn behaviors from their environment. Young foxes learn how to hunt by watching their parents.

3. Traits Can Change in Humans

Suppose you fall off your bike and scrape your knee. After your knee heals, a scar forms. A scar is a new trait.

People's traits are affected by their environment. If people do not eat enough food, they can lose weight. If a child's environment does not have nutritious food, they might not grow very tall.

Like other animals, some traits you have are learned. When you were born, you did not know how to tie your shoes. You learned to tie your shoes when you were young. A few years later, you may have also learned how to ride a bike. These learned behaviors are traits.

Writing is a learned behavior. This child did not know how to write when he was born.

4. Traits Can Change in Plants

Have you ever tried to grow flowers or other plants? What if the plant's environment has too much sunshine? Or not enough sunshine?

The environment can change some traits in plants, too. Plants that get dried out from too much sunshine may turn brown. Plants that do not receive enough sunshine may change color. A plant's color is a trait that can change. The environment can change a plant's color.

Another trait that can change in plants is height. If a plant's environment has enough water and sunshine, that plant might grow very tall. If a plant's environment does not have the right amount of water or sunshine, that plant might not grow very tall. The environment can change a plant's height.

This plant's environment has plenty of water and sunshine. Its environment is helping the plant grow tall.

How Does the Environment Affect Traits?

1. Some Traits Are Not Passed to Offspring   An organism may gain or lose traits during its lifetime. These changes are often caused by the organism's environment. Some traits, like a flamingo's pink feathers, come from its environment.

2. Traits Can Change in Animals   The environment can change the traits of animals. A scar is one example of a trait caused by an animal's environment. Some animals can also learn new behaviors. These behaviors are traits the animal was not born with. The animal learned from its environment.

3. Traits Can Change in Humans   The environment can change the traits of humans. Like other animals, people gain new traits, such as scars or strength. Humans also learn how to do many things that they could not do when they were born, like talking or riding a bike.

4. Traits Can Change in Plants   The environment can change the traits of plants. The amount of sunshine or water can affect a plant's traits. A plant that has the wrong amount of these things in its environment may not grow as tall or produce healthy leaves.

Animal Commuters

Animals that live in cities have some unusual behaviors. You might have seen a cat or dog crossing the street. But have you ever seen one riding a bus?

The bus pulled up to the bus stop and opened its doors. A white cat wearing a purple collar leapt through the doors and crawled under a seat. A few stops later, he got off the bus. "I suppose he is the perfect passenger really—he sits quietly, minds his own business, and then gets off," said a man on the bus.

You know that people can teach animals new behaviors. Dogs can learn to shake hands. Birds can be taught to say words. But animals can also learn to do new things on their own.

Cities are not natural environments. But some city animals have learned behaviors that help them meet their needs. These needs include finding food and shelter.

Animals can learn new behaviors to adapt to a city environment. Some cats that live in cities in England have learned to use their buses and trains.

Some city cats board buses to get food and stay warm.

The bus-riding cat is nicknamed Macavity, and he lives in England. Several days a week, Macavity boards the bus from the same spot. After riding a few blocks, he gets off. His stop is always the same place. Where does he go? No one knows for sure, but there is a restaurant that serves fried fish where he gets off. He probably gets food from this shop. Macavity has learned to use the bus to help him get food.

Another cat in England named Dodger also learned the same trick. Dodger boards the bus by himself from a stop near his owner's house. When the bus reaches that stop again, he gets off. He does this two to three times a week. His owner believes that Dodger likes the warmth of the bus, and he often sits in passengers' laps.

Some stray dogs have learned how to ride the train. They use the train to find food in the city.

Dogs Riding Trains

Cats are not the only animals that catch rides on public transportation. In Moscow, a big city in Russia, trains carry many passengers each day. Some of the passengers are stray dogs.

Stray dogs use the train to find food. Many of the dogs sleep outside the city, but go into the city to eat. So, the stray dogs get on the train each morning and ride into Moscow. Then they return home at night.

How do these dogs know when to get off the train? They might use their powerful sense of smell to find the right stop. They may also remember how long the train ride is to know when to get off. Some may even recognize the name of the stop when it is called. Dogs can learn the sound of words, just as they learn the sound of their own names.

Monkeys on the Metro

In Delhi, a large city in India, thousands of rhesus monkeys roam around freely. They are not easily bothered by people. The monkeys have even learned to beg for food.

Often the monkeys board metro trains in search of food. A metro train is a subway. The monkeys have been known to travel from one station to another looking for food. Some even sit in the seats and hang on to the handrails. At least they are safe passengers!

Cities around the world are growing. As they do, more animals will learn to live in city environments. People will likely bump into more animal commuters. Look out! Soon you might share a seat with a passenger of another species.

Some animals, like this Rhesus monkey, are learning to live in city environments.

How Are Traits Affected by Both Inheritance and the Environment?

Science Vocabulary

genes

These baby geese all look very similar to each other. But as they grow, they will look more different. Some might be bigger than others. Some might have more feathers than others. You will learn how the environment causes organisms in the same species to look different from each other.

NGSS **3-LS3-1.** Analyze and interpret data to provide evidence that plants and animals have traits inherited from parents and that variation of these traits exists in a group of similar organisms. **3-LS3-2.** Use evidence to support the explanation that traits can be influenced by the environment.

LS3.A. • Many characteristics of organisms are inherited from their parents. • Other characteristics result from individuals' interactions with the environment, which can range from diet to learning. Many characteristics involve both inheritance and environment. **LS3.B.** • Different organisms vary in how they look and function because they have different inherited information. • The environment also affects the traits that an organism develops.

Cause and Effect Cause and effect relationships are routinely identified and used to explain change.

 **Constructing Explanations and Designing Solutions**

1. Plants Inherit Genes

You have already learned that some traits can be inherited. Think of an adult rose plant. It has many big, pink flowers. Now think of its offspring, a baby rose plant. Does that baby plant have big, pink flowers? No, it does not. Do you think that baby plant will have flowers when it grows up?

Inherited traits are passed on through *genes*. **Genes** are inherited information that tells offspring what traits to have. That adult rose plant passed on genes to its offspring. Those genes tell the baby plant how to grow flowers when it is older. The baby plant does not have flowers when it sprouts. It grows them when it is older. But the flowers are still an inherited trait. The genes passed to a baby plant from its parents tell the plant what kind of flowers to grow and when.

This baby rose plant has inherited genes to grow flowers. The flowers are an inherited trait.

2. Plant Inheritance and the Environment

Think of a baby rose plant again. It has inherited genes to grow big, pink flowers. Does that mean it will always grow big, pink flowers in its lifetime? No, it does not.

Many traits of plants are affected by both inheritance and the environment. For instance, the rose plant has inherited genes to grow big, pink flowers when it is older. But what if the plant gets a disease from another plant in its environment? The diseased rose plant may only grow brown, unhealthy flowers. The rose plant's flowers are a trait that was affected by inheritance and the plant's environment.

Another baby rose plant may also inherit genes to grow big, pink flowers. If its environment does not have the disease, then the rose plant is healthy. It will grow big, pink flowers. This rose plant has a different trait because its environment is different.

These plants inherited the same genes to make big, pink flowers. But the environment of the plant on the left gave it a disease. That made it grow unhealthy flowers instead.

3. Animals Inherit Genes

Have you ever seen a newborn baby bird? Most baby birds do not have feathers. But most adult birds do! How does a baby bird's body know to grow feathers as it gets older?

Like plants, animals inherit traits that are passed on as genes. For instance, baby birds may not have feathers when they are born. They grow feathers when they are older. Baby birds inherit genes to grow feathers from their parents. Their feathers are an inherited trait.

Another example is a frog's legs. Tadpoles do not have legs when they are born. They grow legs as they grow older and become adults. Tadpoles inherit genes to grow legs from their parents. So, their legs are an inherited trait.

These tadpoles hatched with no legs. But they inherited genes from their parents to grow legs when they are older.

4. Animal Inheritance and the Environment

What is some inherited information that animals can have? Can you think of how the environment might affect them?

Like plants, many traits of animals are affected by inheritance and the environment. One trait that can be affected is size. For instance, a wild piglet may inherit genes that tell it to grow to 50 kg (110 lb). If the piglet does not eat very much food, it may only grow to 30 kg (66 lb). Another wild piglet may inherit genes to grow to 30 kg. If the piglet eats enough food and water, it may grow to 30 kg, too. Both pigs are 30 kg, but they grew up in different environments and inherited different genes. Their size is a trait that is affected by both inheritance and the environment.

These two pigs grew up to be the same size. But they may have inherited different genes and grown up in different environments.

How Are Traits Affected by Both Inheritance and the Environment?

1. Plants Inherit Genes   Inherited traits are passed on to offspring through genes. Baby plants, for example, do not have flowers. But their parents pass on genes for them to grow a certain kind of flower when they are older. Flowers are an example of an inherited trait.

2. Plant Inheritance and the Environment   Many traits in plants are affected by inheritance and the environment. For example, a rose inherits genes to grow flowers of a certain color and size. But if it gets a disease that affects its flowers, they may look different.

3. Animals Inherit Genes   Like plants, animal parents pass on genes to their offspring. When baby birds are first born, they do not have feathers. Young birds inherit genes to grow feathers as they get older. Feathers are another example of an inherited trait.

4. Animal Inheritance and the Environment   Many animal traits are also affected by inheritance and the environment. A pig's size is one example. It inherits genes that tell it to grow to a certain size. But if its environment does not have enough food it may not grow that large.

So You Want to Get a Puppy

A dog's traits are determined by both its genes and the environment. When choosing a family puppy, knowing which breed you want is the first step. Training is the second.

You want a dog that can learn cool tricks. Your dad wants a short-haired dog. Your mom wants a dog that can run with her. How can you choose a puppy that will have all of these traits?

When you get a puppy, you do not know exactly how it will look or act when it is an adult. But you can predict a lot about a dog by its breed. A breed is a group of animals of the same species that are similar in most traits. All dogs belong to the same species. That means that they have a certain number of genes in common. But dogs of a certain breed have even more traits in common. So, if you know a dog's breed, you know what many of its traits will be.

If you pick out a puppy of a certain breed, you can predict what many of its traits will be. Labrador retrievers tend to be friendly and outgoing.

Dachshunds were bred to be helpful to hunters due to their long bodies and short legs.

How Dog Breeds Differ

A Chihuahua can fit in a handbag. A Great Dane is almost as tall as a pony! Dogs come in many different shapes and sizes.

The body shape of some breeds makes them useful for certain jobs. Dachshunds have long bodies and short legs. This makes them very helpful to hunters as they can chase after animals in underground holes. Small dogs, like Pomeranians, can sit comfortably in your lap.

There is also variety in how breeds tend to behave. Some breeds are useful for their behaviors. Border collies tend to guide other animals together. This behavior makes them good at herding sheep. They also have a lot of energy and do not make good lap dogs. Would a border collie be a good fit in your home?

Border collies are good at guiding animals together. This makes them useful for herding sheep.

Crossing Breeds

Each breed of dog has a certain set of traits. A Labrador retriever has short, straight hair, a heavy body, and a broad head. A poodle has curly hair, a thinner body, and a narrow head. These traits come from the dog's genes.

Like other animals, dogs inherit genes from their parents. When two Labradors have offspring, their puppies inherit Labrador traits. When two poodles have puppies, they will have poodle traits.

Maybe you are looking to a get a crossbred dog. A crossbred puppy has a father of one breed and a mother of another breed. Some of the traits come from one breed. Other traits come from the other breed. That's why crossbred puppies don't look exactly like either parent!

A labradoodle has one parent who is a Labrador retriever and one parent who is a poodle. A crossbred dog, like a labradoodle, inherits traits from the breeds of both its parents.

Labrador retriever

Labradoodle

Poodle

A dog's environment can affect how a dog behaves. When you teach a dog how to sit, it learns a new behavior.

Dog Traits and the Environment

Not all of a dog's traits come from genes. Some come from the environment. That's one reason why two dogs of the same breed can be so different from one another.

You might see pictures of poodles that have big hairdos and bare patches on their bodies. They are not born with these traits. Someone has styled their fur to look this way. These traits are a result of the dog's environment and not its genes.

A dog's environment can affect the way it behaves, too. A dog gets the ability to learn from its genes. But the tricks it learns come from its environment. When your new puppy comes home, you will have to teach it to sit, stay, and come to you when you call it. Your puppy will have inherited many of its traits. But *you* will teach it to be a member of your family.

Why Do Some Members of a Species Survive and Not Others?

Science Vocabulary

camouflage

mate

reproduce

survive

Which of these animals do you think will survive? All organisms try to survive and reproduce. But you will learn why not all organisms are able to do this. By observing plants and animals, you can explain which traits help them survive and reproduce.

NGSS

3-LS4-2. Use evidence to construct an explanation for how the variations in characteristics among individuals of the same species may provide advantages in surviving, finding mates, and reproducing.

LS4.B. Sometimes the differences in characteristics between individuals of the same species provide advantages in surviving, finding mates, and reproducing.

Cause and Effect Cause and effect relationships are routinely identified and used to explain change.

Constructing Explanations and Designing Solutions

1. Survival Is Important to Organisms

What if dogs stopped making more dogs? There would be no more puppies on Earth. What would happen to dogs? They would soon disappear.

Organisms **reproduce**, or make more of their own species of organism. Producing offspring makes sure that there will be more members of a species. All living things reproduce.

Being able to *survive* is also important for all organisms. To **survive** means to stay alive. Some animals hunt other animals to survive. Those other animals try to avoid being eaten. For an eagle to survive, it must hunt and eat rabbits. For a rabbit to survive, it must run and hide from eagles.

Plants also try to survive. Plants need light to make food. A plant's leaves grow and move to take in more sunlight.

This jackrabbit needed to run away from the eagle to survive. If it were faster, it might have been able to avoid the eagle.

2. Some Individuals Do Not Survive or Reproduce

Lions live together in groups called prides. Members of the pride work together to hunt and catch prey. They all eat the food. By working together to hunt large prey, individual lions can get more food than they would on their own.

All animals try to survive and reproduce, but some individuals in a group fail. All lions in a pride need to eat to survive. But a small or weak lion may not be strong enough to fight with the other lions for food. An ill or injured lion may not be able to survive long enough to reproduce.

Some tomato plants in a garden will grow fruit. Other tomato plants may not. Insects or other animals may eat the leaves. The plant could become weak and die. It might not be able to grow seeds to make new plants.

This tomato plant may not reproduce, or it may produce fewer offspring. Its fruits are being eaten by insects.

The neck length of a giraffe is a trait that varies among individuals. Giraffes with longer necks are able to reach more food than giraffes with shorter necks.

3. An Animal Has Traits That Help It Survive

Think about an octopus. What traits do you think it might have to help it survive?

Some individual animals have different traits that help them survive. For example, most species of octopus have *camouflage*. **Camouflage** is when an animal's color makes it hard to see. An octopus with good camouflage might be able to hide from sharks that want to eat it. Then it will survive. An octopus with worse camouflage may get eaten.

The length of a giraffe's neck is another trait that is different among individuals. Giraffes eat leaves from shrubs and trees. If a brush fire killed shrubs close to the ground, the giraffes would have only the tree leaves for food. Giraffes with longer necks may get more food than other giraffes. Those with shorter necks will not be able to reach as much food and they may not survive.

4. An Animal Has Traits That Help It Reproduce

Think about a group of lion cubs. The cubs' parents reproduced to make those offspring. But not all adult lions reproduce.

To reproduce, most animals must find a *mate*. A **mate** is another animal of the same species with which the animal can reproduce. One adult lion cannot reproduce. It needs to find another lion that can be its mate. But how do animals find mates?

Different individual animals find mates because of different traits they have. Males of some species have traits to help attract a mate. Male peacocks have large, colorful tail feathers. To attract a mate, male peacocks will raise their feathers and move them around. This is a trait that helps male peacocks find mates. If one male does not have these traits, he may not be able to reproduce.

This is a male peacock. He uses his large, bright feathers to attract mates so he can reproduce.

5. A Plant Has Traits That Help It Survive

An animal can run away or hide from enemies. Plants cannot run away from danger, but they have other traits that help them survive.

Some individual plants survive because they have different traits. Some plants have traits that keep animals from eating them. Many species of rose have stems with hard, sharp points called prickles. Prickles are painful to some animals, so they stay away. Rose plants with larger prickles will likely keep more animals away. A rose plant with the trait of fewer, smaller, or softer prickles may get eaten.

Some plants have traits that help them fight diseases. Elm trees can get a disease that kills them. Some elm trees have a trait that helps them fight off the disease and survive. Some do not have that trait and the disease kills them.

This rose plant has the trait of prickles. Prickles keep some animals from eating the rose, making it more likely to survive.

6. A Plant Has Traits That Help It Reproduce

Have you ever looked closely at a strawberry? Strawberries are covered with seeds. Even though all strawberries are covered with seeds, not all strawberry plants will reproduce.

To reproduce, a strawberry plant needs at least one of its seeds to grow into a new plant. For this to happen, a seed has to move away from its parent plant. One way this could happen is if a bird eats a strawberry and moves its seeds to new soil.

Some strawberry plants have different traits from other strawberry plants. Some have bigger berries. Some have sweeter berries. Strawberry plants with brighter or sweeter berries attract more birds. The seeds on these berries are more likely to grow into new plants. So, some plants of a species have traits that help them reproduce more than others.

This strawberry plant has big, sweet, red fruit. Having these large berries is a trait that will help this plant reproduce, since the fruits will attract more animals.

Why Do Some Members of a Species Survive and Not Others?

1. Survival Is Important to Organisms   All organisms try to survive and reproduce. When an organism reproduces, it makes more of its own kind. To reproduce, a plant or animal must survive long enough in its environment.

2. Some Individuals Do Not Survive or Reproduce   Individuals have different traits from other individuals of their same species. Some of these traits may make it harder to survive or reproduce.

3. An Animal Has Traits That Help It Survive   Animals of one kind can have different traits. These individual traits help some animals of one kind survive when others do not. Some traits that help animals survive are camouflage and size.

4. An Animal Has Traits That Help It Reproduce   Differences in traits help some animals find mates more easily than others. One trait that helps animals find mates is bright colors.

5. A Plant Has Traits That Help It Survive   Plants of one kind also have different traits. Some of these traits can help some plants survive better than others. For example, some traits help plants fight disease and protect themselves.

6. A Plant Has Traits That Help It Reproduce   Differing traits help some plants reproduce more than others. Some of these traits are tasty fruits, bright flowers, and seeds that can move very far.

Animal Spy Cameras

The powerful black bear stands up on its hind legs. It is the size of an adult human and has sharp teeth and claws. The bear rubs its back against a nearby tree. "Excuse me," you ask, "May I measure you and take a few hair samples?"

Black bears rub against trees to leave a scent. Scientists place hair traps on the tree to collect a bear's fur.

You definitely should not come up to a black bear and ask such a favor. Neither should a scientist. But scientists need to gather data about these wild animals. How can they do this safely?

Some teams of scientists use tools called hair traps to safely keep track of wild bears. The hair traps are pieces of barbed wire nailed to tree trunks. When the bear rubs against the tree to leave its scent, the wire catches some of its hair. But the wire does not hurt the bear. Scientists come by after the bear has left and collect the hair. Then they test the hair to find out more about the bear it belonged to.

This picture of a black bear was taken by a camera trap in Grand Canyon National Park.

Sensing When to Click

Scientists also use cameras to safely collect data about animals like bears. These cameras do not take pictures at every moment. They have a sensor that can tell when an animal visits. This tool is called a camera trap.

Some camera traps use a trip wire, or a wire that is pulled tight between two trees. When an animal walks up against it, the tripwire pulls on the camera and turns it on. Other cameras use light sensors. When the animal passes through and blocks a beam of invisible light, it turns on the camera. So, the camera takes pictures only when the animals come by.

Camera traps let scientists watch animals from hard-to-reach places. They take pictures of animals that live in remote areas. They also take pictures of animals that come out only at night.

An Animal's Point of View

Using cameras to spy on animals is not always about being safe. Scientists want to know how animals act in nature. Suppose a wild animal sees a human following it. Or imagine it sees strange tools near its home. The animal might act differently.

Scientists sometimes have animals wear cameras. Scientists have put cameras on birds. The camera records what a bird sees while it moves around. They show the bird's point of view. The bird must first get used to wearing the camera. Then, it can act naturally. It can go places it normally goes. It can do what it normally does. In this way, scientists can learn more about the bird without changing how it acts.

Scientists develop tools to learn more about the lives of animals. Scientists have used underwater cameras to learn about the lives of penguins.

Data-Gathering Backpack

Animals can also carry other tools. These tools can gather other kinds of data.

In one investigation, scientists outfitted penguins with cases on their backs attached with straps. Inside the cases were cameras and tools that took measurements. They could collect data while the penguin dove below the surface of the ocean. They could measure how many meters down the penguin dove. Sometimes scientists place tags on the backs of penguins that send data to a satellite. Scientists can learn about how penguins move and where they get food. All these data helped scientists find patterns that they use to better understand penguins and their life cycles.

Scientists continue to develop new tools. These tools help them learn more about the secret lives of different animals.

Scientists continue to develop new tools to learn about the life cycle of different animals. This Adelie penguin is wearing a tool that scientists put on its back.

What Are the Life Cycles of Plants?

Science Vocabulary

flower

fruit

life cycle

life span

seed

This fruit did not always look this way. You will learn how a plant changes as it goes through its life cycle. These changes during a life cycle form a pattern. The amount of time it takes to complete a life cycle differs from one type of plant to another.

NGSS

3-LS1-1. Develop models to describe that organisms have unique and diverse life cycles but all have in common birth, growth, reproduction, and death.

LS1.B. Reproduction is essential to the continued existence of every kind of organism. Plants and animals have unique and diverse life cycles.

Patterns Patterns of change can be used to make predictions.

Developing and Using Models

1. Plants Have Different Life Spans

Suppose you are walking through the woods. You see some plants that are alive. They have green leaves and bright flowers. You also see plants that are dead, like a tree that has fallen down.

A **life span** is the typical amount of time that members of a species live, from birth to death. Different species have different life spans. During an organism's life span, it grows, develops, and tries to reproduce. For example, common sunflowers live for less than one year. Their life span is one growing season. Some other plant species have longer life spans. Apple trees, for example, have life spans of 100 years. Some trees have even longer life spans. Redwood trees can live for over 1,000 years!

These common sunflowers have a life span of only one growing season. These adult plants will all die before the end of the year.

2. Plants Reproduce

Think of the different flowers you have seen. Many plants produce flowers. What do flowers do for the plant?

A **flower** is the part in some plants where *seeds* are made. A **seed** is a small, protected part of a plant that can grow into an adult offspring. All plants need to reproduce. Plants that grow flowers do this by producing seeds. To grow seeds, flowers need *pollen*. Pollen is also grown in flowers, but it usually moves from one flower to another. Wind and insects can move pollen. Pollen sticks to insects when they land on flowers. The insect may fly to another flower of the same species. Some of its pollen will rub off there.

After pollen gets to the flower, a *fruit* develops and seeds form inside of it. A **fruit** is the part of a plant that surrounds and protects a seed. Some flowering plants have juicy fruits, like an apple. Others have dry fruits, like dandelions.

Each of these seeds is able to grow into a new plant. The fruits and their seeds all grew from flowers.

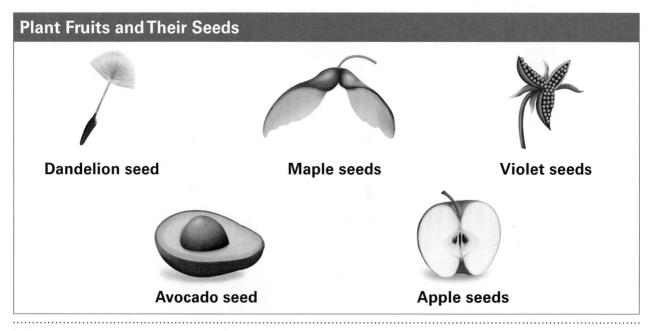

Plant Fruits and Their Seeds

Dandelion seed　　　**Maple seeds**　　　**Violet seeds**

Avocado seed　　　**Apple seeds**

3. Sunflowers Have a Life Cycle

When scientists observe how living things grow, they look for patterns. A *pattern* is something, such as a series of changes, that repeats.

Plants go through a series of changes as they grow. The pattern of changes that a member of a species goes through during its lifetime is called a **life cycle**.

Common sunflower plants go through different stages in their life cycle. Each sunflower begins its life as a seed. If the seed has enough water and is warm enough, it sprouts into a seedling. Over time, the seedling can grow into an adult plant. Adult sunflower plants can make flowers. With enough sunshine and water, the flowers can make new seeds. Each sunflower seed is surrounded by a tiny dry fruit that protects the seed inside. Finally, after a common sunflower makes new seeds, it dies. A sunflower's life cycle is a pattern that its offspring repeat.

A common sunflower plant goes through its full life cycle in less than a year. At the end of the growing season, it dies and drops seeds that begin the life cycle again.

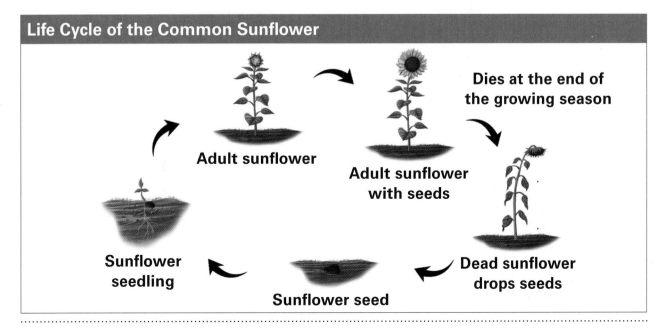

Life Cycle of the Common Sunflower

Adult sunflower

Adult sunflower with seeds

Dies at the end of the growing season

Dead sunflower drops seeds

Sunflower seed

Sunflower seedling

4. Apple Trees Have a Life Cycle

When you last ate an apple, did you see the seeds inside? Those tiny seeds can grow into big apple trees if the conditions are right.

Apple trees go through a similar life cycle to sunflowers. An apple tree also starts as a seed. If the seed has enough water and sunshine, it will sprout into a seedling. Over many years, the seedling might grow into an adult plant. In spring, leaves and flowers grow on adult apple trees. Next, the flowers make seeds and apples, a fruit that surrounds the new seeds. Unlike a sunflower, an apple tree's fruit is large and juicy. The seeds inside the new apples can grow into new apple trees. The new apple trees will then go through the life cycle again. Unlike sunflowers, adult apple trees can survive to reproduce many times before they die.

An apple tree makes fruits with seeds, but not until it has grown for several years. The adult apple tree can survive for many years and make new fruit each year.

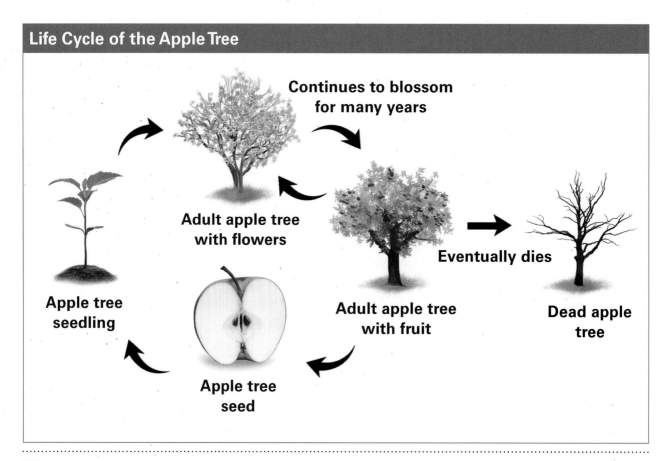

Life Cycle of the Apple Tree

Continues to blossom for many years

Adult apple tree with flowers

Eventually dies

Apple tree seedling

Adult apple tree with fruit

Dead apple tree

Apple tree seed

What Are the Life Cycles of Plants?

1. Plants Have Different Life Spans Different plants have different life spans. A life span is how long most organisms of a certain kind live for. Many plants live for only one year, like sunflowers. Other plants, like apple trees and redwoods, can live much longer.

2. Plants Reproduce Many plants reproduce using seeds. Seeds have a tiny plant inside that can grow into an adult plant. Some seeds develop inside flowers, after the flowers receive pollen. Most seeds have fruit that surrounds and protects them.

3. Sunflowers Have a Life Cycle Organisms go through a pattern of changes called a life cycle. Different species have life cycles with different patterns. Sunflowers have a life cycle with several stages: a seed, a seedling, an adult plant, and an adult plant with new seeds. After the common sunflower makes seeds, it dies.

4. Apple Trees Have a Life Cycle An apple tree's life cycle goes through similar stages to a sunflower's. Apple seeds grow inside apples after the apple tree's flowers receive pollen from other flowers. These seeds can grow into new apple trees. But apple trees can live for many years and reproduce many times.

Getting into the Treetops

Scientists who study the life cycles of plants and animals often study them in the wild. For some scientists, this can mean a trip into the treetops. How can technology help scientists explore high above the ground?

A scientist stands in a tree 30 m (about 98 ft) off the rainforest floor. He checks his harness. A rope tied to the harness connects him to a branch of the tree. He also wears a helmet to protect his head. Carefully, he reaches out to collect pollen from the beautiful flower of a plant called an *orchid*.

A rainforest is an area with dense trees and lots of rain. The trees can be taller than 55 m (over 180 ft)! Orchids, birds, and other wildlife often spend their whole lives in these trees. So, scientists who study the rainforest must often go high up into the trees.

To reach rainforest birds high up in the treetops, a scientist must use a harness, helmet, ropes, and other climbing gear.

The ropes and harnesses that scientists use to climb up into rainforest trees are examples of technology. They must be strong enough to hold a person.

Another kind of technology helps scientists move from one tree to another very quickly. This is called a zip line. A zip line is a cable stretched between two trees or towers. One end of the line is higher than the other. You can hook equipment, like a harness, to the cable. The hook slides freely along the zip line. So, when you hang from the hook at the higher end of the line, you will slide downwards. You can slide so fast that it feels almost like flying!

Do climbing and zipping through a forest sound like fun? If so, then you might want to become a scientist who studies the rainforest.

Orchids are flowering plants that live on the bark of rainforest trees.

A zip line lets you speed through the rainforest from tree to tree without touching the ground.

What Are the Life Cycles of Animals with Backbones?

Science Vocabulary

metamorphosis

vertebrate

What do mammals, birds, fish, reptiles, and amphibians have in common? You will find out how their skeletons are alike. While they all have life cycles, there are differences between these groups of animals. You can study patterns in a life cycle to predict how an animal will change as it grows up.

NGSS **3-LS1-1.** Develop models to describe that organisms have unique and diverse life cycles but all have in common birth, growth, reproduction, and death.

LS1.B. Reproduction is essential to the continued existence of every kind of organism. Plants and animals have unique and diverse life cycles.

Patterns Patterns of change can be used to make predictions.

Developing and Using Models

1. Some Animals Have Backbones

Think of animals you know. Some may have fur. Others have feathers or scales. If you have ever touched the back of an animal with fur, feathers, or scales, you may have felt a line of bones under its skin. This is its backbone.

Animals can be grouped by whether or not they have backbones. Animals that have backbones are called **vertebrates**. Vertebrates are classified into seven, smaller animal groups. Mammals, reptiles, and birds are vertebrates. So are fish and amphibians. Cats, elephants, and humans are mammals. Snakes, lizards, and turtles are reptiles. Parrots and ducks are birds. Goldfish and sharks are fish. Frogs and salamanders are amphibians.

Cats are vertebrates. If you pet a cat, you can feel its backbone.

Bats are mammals that can fly. Like other mammals, they feed their young with milk. Elephants are very large mammals. They live on land and are covered with small hairs.

2. Mammals Have a Similar Life Cycle

What do cats, dogs, elephants, and humans have in common? They are all mammals! Mammals have some traits in common, and they also have similar life cycles.

Mammals are vertebrates that can produce milk for their young. They are also covered in hair. Mammals keep their bodies at a steady temperature. Their body temperature stays the same, even when the temperature of their environment changes. That means that a bear keeps itself cool in the summer and warm in the winter.

Most mammals live on land. But some mammals live in water. Whales spend their entire lives in water. They come up to the water's surface to breathe air. Some mammals, like river otters, live on both land and water.

Most baby mammals grow and develop inside of their mother's body. Each mammal species develops in its own amount of time. Baby mice develop in about three weeks. It takes more than a year and a half for baby elephants to develop.

After baby mammals have developed, the mother gives birth. Their parents take care of them while they are young. When young mammals grow into adults, they can reproduce. The cycle begins again. Many mammals can reproduce several times during their lives.

Different mammals have different life spans. Harp seals can live for 35 years. Most mice only live for about two years. But the shortest mammal life span is under one year for some mouse species. Bowhead whales can live for almost 200 years!

Mice develop inside their mother's body until they are born. Their mothers take care of them when they are babies, until they grow into adults.

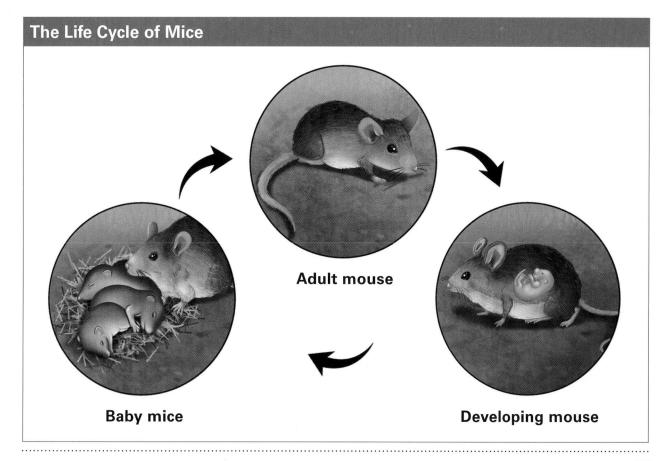

The Life Cycle of Mice

Adult mouse

Baby mice

Developing mouse

3. Bird, Reptile, and Fish Life Cycles Are Similar

Can you think of something that birds, reptiles, and fish have in common? They are all vertebrates, and they all lay eggs! Their life cycles are similar but not exactly the same.

All bird life cycles begin with an egg. A baby bird grows and develops inside of the egg, which has a hard shell. Most of the time, adult birds keep the eggs warm and protect them while the baby birds develop.

When baby birds are grown and developed enough, the eggs hatch. Most parents feed and protect the babies until they can leave the nest, and even afterwards. When the baby birds grow into adults, they can lay their own eggs, starting the life cycle over again.

Different birds can also have different life spans. Mourning doves only live for about a year and a half, while many parrots can live for over 50!

This is a young robin. Like many young birds, it cannot fly or feed itself. So, its parents take care of it.

Most reptiles have a life cycle that also starts with an egg. The shell develops around the egg inside of the mother's body. The young reptiles that hatch look like small adults. Some young snakes grow to adult snakes in about a year. Adult snakes can then lay new eggs, repeating their life cycle.

Fish are also vertebrates that hatch from eggs. Fish life cycles take place in water. Some fish live in salty oceans. Others live in freshwater. Most fish eggs are laid in water but, unlike bird and reptile eggs, fish eggs do not have a shell. Adult fish that survive long enough can lay new eggs, starting their life cycle over again.

The changes that birds, reptiles, and fish go through during their lives form patterns. There are many similarities between their life cycles.

Unlike most baby birds, this baby turtle can take care of itself as soon as it hatches. It is able to swim and crawl.

4. Amphibians Go Through Metamorphosis

Frogs, toads, and salamanders are amphibians. How does a baby amphibian differ from an adult?

Amphibians have life cycles that are different from other vertebrates. Amphibians go through *metamorphosis*. **Metamorphosis** is a large change in body shape that happens during the life cycles of some animal species.

Adult female frogs lay eggs without shells in water. Tadpoles hatch from the eggs. Tadpoles have a tail and breathe underwater. They do not look like their parents. The tadpoles grow larger and start to go through metamorphosis. Four legs grow, and the tail disappears. The tadpole develops into a small frog that breathes air and can live on land. Soon, the frog can reproduce and the life cycle repeats.

Frog eggs are laid underwater and eventually hatch into tadpoles. Tadpoles also live underwater but will go through metamorphosis and become an adult.

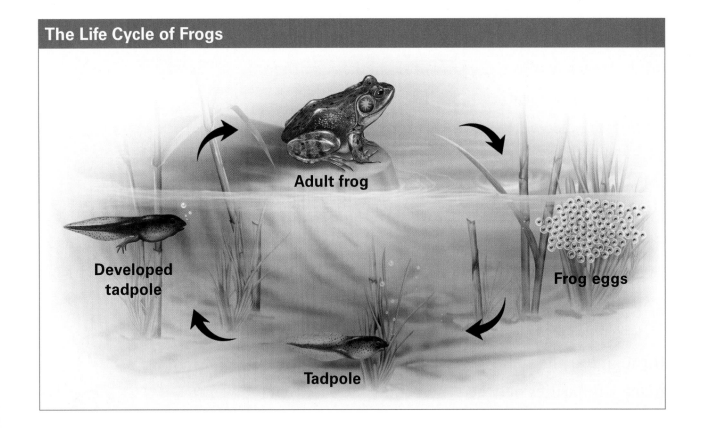

The Life Cycle of Frogs

Adult frog

Frog eggs

Developed tadpole

Tadpole

What Are the Life Cycles of Animals with Backbones?

1. Some Animals Have Backbones There are many different species of animals. Some species have backbones. Animals with backbones are grouped together as vertebrates. Vertebrates include mammals, birds, fish, reptiles, and amphibians.

2. Mammals Have a Similar Life Cycle Mammals are vertebrates that can produce milk for their young. They are also covered in hair. Most mammals go through a similar life cycle. Most mammal babies grow and develop inside their mothers before they are born.

3. Bird, Reptile, and Fish Life Cycles Are Similar Birds, reptiles, and fish have similar life cycles. Their life cycles start with an egg. Almost all kinds of birds take care of their young after they hatch, but most reptiles and fish do not.

4. Amphibians Go Through Metamorphosis Amphibian life cycles are very different from those of other vertebrates. Amphibians go through metamorphosis, which is a very large change in body shape. So, most baby amphibians do not look like their parents at first.

A Passion for Chimps

Chimps and humans are both mammals. They have similar life cycles. They are also alike in many other ways.

The scientist comes out on stage. As the applause dies down, she makes a small *o* shape with her lips. Suddenly, she calls out in a shrill voice, "Oo oo oo oo oo OOO oo OOO oo OOO!"

The scientist is English biologist Jane Goodall. She explains that this sound means "good evening" in chimpanzee. She knows this because she has been studying chimp behavior for more than 50 years.

Through years of watching these animals in the wild, Goodall has learned much about them. She has learned how they get their food, what their families are like, and how they talk to each other. Her discoveries have changed the way that people view chimps.

Jane Goodall's work has shown that humans have more in common with chimps than you might think.

Chimps use sticks to catch insects that they eat.

Observing in the Field

As a young woman, Jane Goodall did not go to school to study science. Instead, she traveled to Africa. While there, she met a scientist who hired her to help him. He sent her to study wild chimps in the East African country of Tanzania.

Through watching the chimps from a hidden place, she made a discovery. At the time, people thought that chimps only ate fruit and vegetables. But Goodall saw that they also ate meat.

Soon after, she made another important discovery. She hid herself near a termite mound where she knew chimps came to eat. She watched two chimps peel the leaves off of sticks. Then they poked the sticks into the mound. When they pulled the sticks out, they were covered with delicious termites. The animals had made and used tools to get their food!

Goodall observed the lives of many chimps to answer her scientific questions. She discovered that chimps are more like humans than scientists thought.

Searching for Answers

Scientists used to think that only humans used tools. Goodall's discovery showed that chimps make and use tools like humans do. She wondered if there were other ways that chimps were like humans.

Goodall knew she would have to learn how to think and speak like a scientist if she wanted to prove her ideas to others. She went to school to learn how scientists study nature. Scientists learn about the world by asking questions. Then they make observations to answer those questions. Using this way of learning, Goodall continued to study chimps.

She asked many questions. Do chimps have unique personalities? Can they show kindness? Do they fight? She watched many chimps to find answers to these questions.

Goodall's research showed that chimps were like humans in other ways. She discovered that chimps help each other. She observed two male chimps help orphaned chimps. They let the orphans sleep in their nests and took care of them. Goodall also saw conflict between the chimps. She saw that sometimes different groups of chimps would fight each other.

More and more scientists studied chimps in the wild. They started meeting to discuss their findings. A very large meeting happened after Goodall had been studying chimps for 25 years. The scientists learned a lot from each other. But some of the news was sad. They realized that wild chimpanzees were becoming threatened with going extinct. So, Goodall became determined to protect the chimps she had come to know so well!

Goodall's discoveries have inspired other scientists to protect threatened wild animals, like chimpanzees.

What Are the Life Cycles of Animals Without Backbones?

Science Vocabulary

exoskeleton

invertebrate

larva

nymph

Some animals, like this grasshopper, do not have backbones. These animals are called invertebrates. You will discover that certain invertebrates go through metamorphosis during their life cycles. But other invertebrates do not. Scientists look for patterns in invertebrate life cycles when studying new species.

NGSS **3-LS1-1.** Develop models to describe that organisms have unique and diverse life cycles but all have in common birth, growth, reproduction, and death.

LS1.B. Reproduction is essential to the continued existence of every kind of organism. Plants and animals have unique and diverse life cycles.

Patterns Patterns of change can be used to make predictions.

 **Developing and Using Models**

1. Some Animals Do Not Have Backbones

What do spiders, honeybees, and crabs all have in common? They all do not have backbones.

Animals without backbones are called **invertebrates**. Most animal species on Earth are invertebrates. Many invertebrates, such as insects, have a hard body covering called an **exoskeleton** instead of bones. Exoskeletons protect the soft insides of most invertebrates. However, exoskeletons cannot grow. So, many invertebrates shed them and grow new ones as they grow larger.

Not all invertebrates have exoskeletons, though. For example, octopuses are invertebrates. They are able to move through spaces that are much smaller than their bodies. They can do this because they do not have a skeleton.

Invertebrates are animals without backbones. Insects have exoskeletons, like one on the left which was shed by a cicada. An octopus, shown on the right, has no skeleton at all.

2. Butterflies Go Through Metamorphosis

You have probably seen butterflies near flowers. Some butterflies are brightly colored. Some have patterns on their wings.

You may have also seen a young butterfly. It does not look like an adult butterfly. It does not have wings or legs like the adult's. Like amphibians, most insects go through metamorphosis. They go through a large change in body shape during their life cycle. The changes many insects go through form a pattern.

The life cycle of butterflies has four stages. It starts with an egg. An adult female butterfly lays eggs with thin shells on a plant leaf.

A wormlike creature hatches from the egg. This second stage in the the life cycle of many invertebrates is called a **larva**. A butterfly larva, also called a *caterpillar*, looks nothing like its parents.

A butterfly's life cycle has four stages. After it becomes an adult, the butterfly can lay eggs, and the life cycle will repeat.

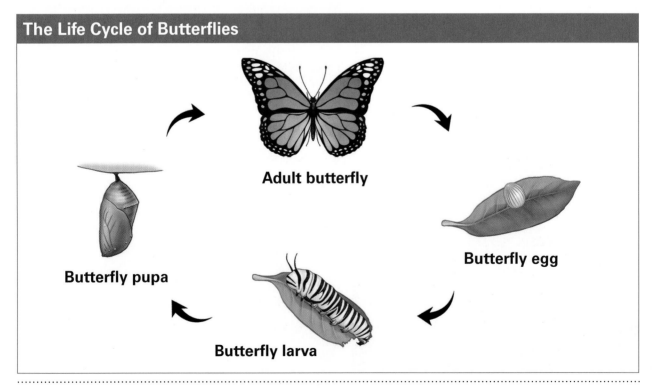

The Life Cycle of Butterflies

Adult butterfly

Butterfly egg

Butterfly larva

Butterfly pupa

This is a new monarch butterfly pupa. The pupa will go through metamorphosis and become an adult.

A butterfly larva spends almost all its time eating and growing. It must grow a new exoskeleton many times because the old ones become too small.

The last time a larva sheds, its body shape changes. Now it is called a *pupa*. A pupa is the third stage in the life cycle of butterflies and some other insects. A pupa does not eat, and it stays in one place. Inside the pupa, an adult butterfly is taking shape. Wings and legs develop. The pupa goes through rapid metamorphosis. It becomes an adult insect.

The final stage in the life cycle of butterflies is the adult. When it is ready, the adult butterfly breaks out of its pupa case. Then it looks for a mate so it can reproduce, and the cycle begins again. Most adult butterflies live six to eight weeks. But some live for only a few days, and some live for many months.

This is an adult dragonfly. Adult dragonflies live near fresh water so they can reproduce and find food.

3. Dragonflies Go Through Metamorphosis

You may have seen dragonflies flying quickly through the air. Dragonflies are insects. Dragonfly bodies may be many colors, including green, blue, and purple. They have long, narrow wings that often have clear windows. Dragonflies live near fresh water, such as ponds, lakes, and streams. They need to be near water to carry out their life cycles.

Dragonflies also go through metamorphosis, but their life cycle is a little different from a butterfly's. The life cycle of a dragonfly has three stages instead of four. A female adult dragonfly lays eggs with thin shells underwater in a pond. She often lays them on the stems of underwater plants. The eggs are the first stage of the dragonfly's life cycle.

In a few weeks, baby dragonflies called *nymphs* hatch out of the eggs. **Nymphs** are young insects that go through gradual metamorphosis. Nymphs are the second stage of a dragonfly's life cycle. They do not look exactly like adult dragonflies. Nymphs do not have wings and cannot fly. They live underwater while they grow and develop. Nymphs hunt and eat insects in water. As nymphs grow, they shed their exoskeleton and grow a new, larger one many times. Sometimes this stage takes many years.

Once a nymph is fully grown, it crawls up the stem of a plant and out of the water. It finishes its metamorphosis by shedding its skin to become an adult dragonfly. Adult dragonflies have wings and do not live underwater anymore. Many adult dragonflies have a life span of about two months. So, they must find mates quickly to reproduce.

Adult dragonflies lay eggs underwater. When a nymph hatches, it begins to grow and change. When the nymph changes into an adult, the metamorphosis is finished.

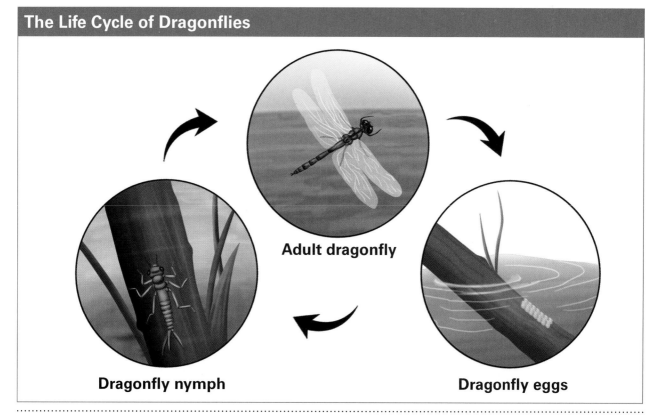

The Life Cycle of Dragonflies

Adult dragonfly

Dragonfly nymph

Dragonfly eggs

4. Lobster Life Cycles

Insects are not the only kinds of invertebrates. Crabs, crayfish, and lobsters are, too. How do these animals compare?

Crabs, crayfish, and lobsters have exoskeletons, just like insects. They also go through metamorphosis. A lobster's life cycle begins with a small soft egg. Thousands of eggs stick to the bottom of the female lobster's tail until they hatch. When an egg hatches, the larva swims near the ocean's surface for a few weeks. As it grows, the larva sheds its exoskeleton many times. After some time, it sinks to the ocean floor where it lives for the rest of its life. As adult lobsters, the females can lay their own eggs, repeating the life cycle. Lobsters have a life span of about 50 years!

A lobster's life cycle has three stages. The eggs ride on the adult female's body. The larva molts many times before it becomes an adult.

The Life Cycle of Lobsters

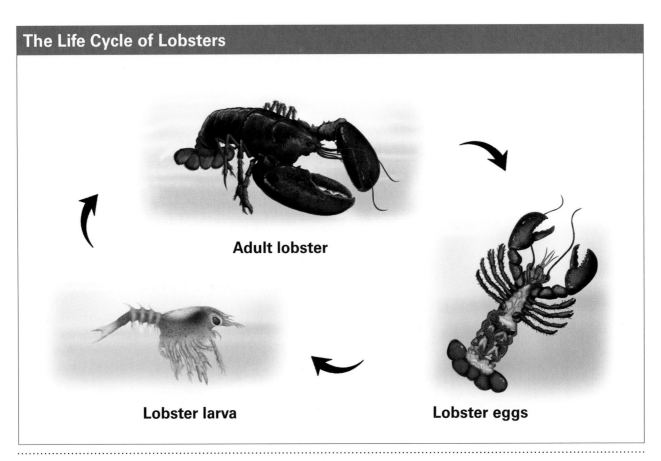

Adult lobster

Lobster larva

Lobster eggs

What Are the Life Cycles of Animals Without Backbones?

1. Some Animals Do Not Have Backbones   Animals that do not have backbones are called invertebrates. Instead of having a skeleton inside their bodies, some have an exoskeleton on the outside. Insects, lobsters, crabs, and octopuses are examples of invertebrates.

2. Butterflies Go Through Metamorphosis   Butterfly life cycles have four stages. The first is a butterfly egg and the second is a larva, or caterpillar. The third is a pupa, and the fourth is an adult butterfly. A young butterfly goes through rapid metamorphosis to look like its parents.

3. Dragonflies Go Through Metamorphosis   Dragonfly life cycles have three stages. The first is a dragonfly egg, the second is a nymph, and the third is an adult dragonfly. During its metamorphosis, a dragonfly nymph slowly changes into an adult.

4. Lobster Life Cycles   Lobster life cycles have three stages. The first is a lobster egg, the second is a lobster larva, and the third is an adult lobster. Lobsters spend their whole lives in the ocean. But they live in different parts of it throughout their life cycle.

Immortal Jellyfish

All living things eventually get old and die. Or do they? One kind of animal may have figured out how to live forever.

The adult jellyfish has lived a full life. It is old now. Even its babies have grown up and had babies of their own. Over time, the jellyfish has changed. And now it is changing again…into a tiny baby!

This life story is actually true for a certain species of jellyfish. The *immortal jellyfish* is an invertebrate that lives in the sea. As an adult, it is no bigger than the end of your finger. It may be small, but it has a special power.

When people say that something is "immortal," they mean it can live forever. The immortal jellyfish does not have to die like other animals. This is because an adult jellyfish can go through its life cycle over and over again.

This adult jellyfish may be old, but it can live more than one life cycle. It can change back into the form it had at a younger stage.

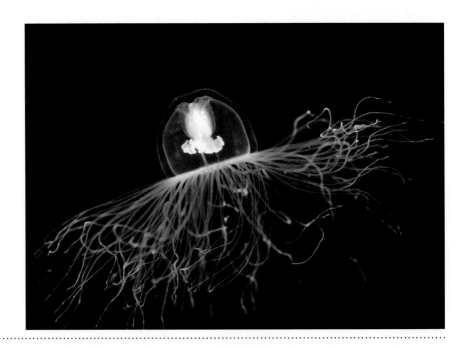

Aging Backwards

Other species of jellyfish have a life cycle that starts with an egg. The egg grows into a larva. The larva sticks itself onto something hard, like a rock or shell. There it becomes a polyp. This stage of the jellyfish looks almost like a plant. Part of it grows, falls off, and swims away. This young jellyfish grows until it becomes an adult. The adult can make eggs, which can start a new cycle. The adult eventually gets old and dies.

The immortal jellyfish has a special trick. When times get tough, the adult can change. If it cannot get enough food or if it gets hurt, it does not have to die. Instead, it can become a group of polyps again. Each of these polyps can grow and become an adult jellyfish. You could say that the jellyfish aged backwards!

Most jellyfish die after they reach the adult stage. But immortal jellyfish can age backwards by changing back into polyps.

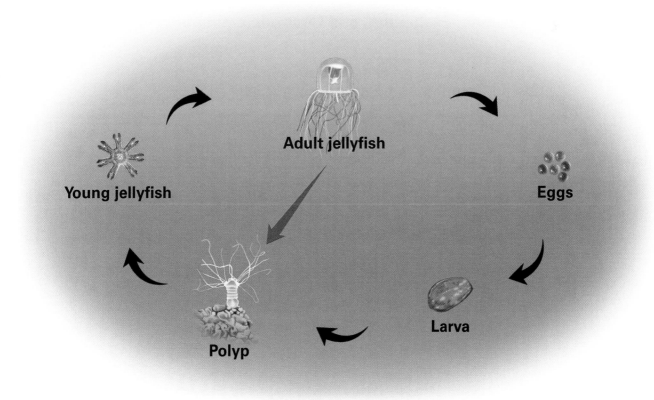

Young jellyfish

Adult jellyfish

Eggs

Larva

Polyp

Science and Engineering Resources

In Science and Engineering Resources, you will learn how to conduct safe investigations using the skills scientists and engineers use, called "practices." You will also learn how to use metric units and measurement tools.

So, what are science and engineering? *Science* is a way of understanding the natural world. Science involves asking questions and gathering evidence. It also involves constructing models and explanations. Science explanations depend on evidence. This evidence must be able to be observed or measured. But as scientists make new discoveries, scientific understandings can change.

Engineering is a way to solve real-world problems. Engineers use their understanding of science to do this. Engineering solutions include a new way of doing something, a new machine, or new structures. Engineering solutions are always changing as engineers test and improve their designs and apply new scientific ideas.

Science Safety

Science investigations are fun. Use these rules to keep yourself and your classmates safe before, during, and after an investigation.

Classroom Science Safety

✓ Wear safety goggles when needed to protect your eyes.

✓ Wear safety gloves when needed to protect your skin.

✓ Wear protective aprons when needed.

✓ Tie back long hair and loose clothing so that they do not touch investigation materials.

✓ Keep tables and desks cleared except for investigation materials.

✓ Carry and handle equipment safely to avoid accidents.

✓ Handle living things with care and respect to protect them and yourself.

✓ Do not eat, drink, or place anything in your mouth during science investigations.

✓ When you work in a team, make sure all members of the team follow safety rules.

✓ Tell your teacher right away if materials spill or break.

✓ Tell your teacher right away if someone gets injured.

✓ Place leftover materials and waste where your teacher tells you to.

✓ Clean up your work area when finished.

✓ Wash your hands with soap and water after cleaning up.

✓ Know your school's safety rules for classroom behavior and follow them.

Outdoor Science Safety

✓ Wear clothing that is good for walking on wet, rocky, or rough ground.

✓ Wear clothes and a hat to protect you from ticks, insects, sun, wind, and rain. It is best to wear shoes that cover the whole foot, have low-heels, and have non-skid soles.

✓ Wear sunscreen if your class plans to be outdoors for more than a few minutes.

✓ Check the weather and sky. Go indoors if lightning may be nearby.

✓ Do not touch plants or animals, alive or dead, without your teacher's permission. Know what plants and animals to be careful of in your area.

✓ Some things are poisonous when eaten. Never taste or eat anything you find outdoors without permission.

✓ Wash your hands with soap and water after any outdoor science activity.

✓ Make sure an adult brings along a first-aid kit.

Planning Investigations

✓ Choose materials that are safe to use.

✓ Plan how you will handle the materials safely.

✓ Include safety steps when writing your procedure.

✓ Always get your teacher's permission before carrying out your investigation plan.

Science and Engineering Practices in Action

Asking Questions and Defining Problems

Questions about the world drive science. A science investigation tries to answer a question. So, a scientist must be able to ask good questions. Questions can be based on observations. For example, "Why do some of my plants grow taller than others?" They can also be based on models, such as the question "Why do most habitats have more living things that make their own food than living things that eat food?" Scientists also ask really big questions like "What happened at the beginning of the universe?"

Asking Scientific Questions

There are many different kinds of questions. One kind is a scientific question. This is question with a definite answer that can be learned through investigation. A question like "Which color is the prettiest?" is not a scientific question. Each person can have their own opinion. So, all answers are correct. But "Which of these two glue recipes makes the strongest glue?" is a scientific question. This is because it has a definite answer.

These students are working to answer a scientific question. They want to know which glue recipe makes the strongest glue. So, they glued a plastic bag to a craft stick. Now they are adding washers to the bag to see how many it can hold.

Questions are also important to engineers. An engineer might ask, "Why did that bridge collapse in the earthquake?" or "Which material is best for a raincoat?"

The goal of engineering is to solve problems to make life better for people. They solve problems by building things or finding new ways to use things. But first they must define the problem they are trying to solve. Asking questions is important for defining problems. Then they can determine how good their solutions are.

Engineers might ask why a bridge collapsed during an earthquake.

Defining a Problem

Defining a problem has two parts. The first is defining the criteria for a successful solution. The *criteria* are the things the solution needs to do. Suppose you are designing a magnetic latch for a box. One of the criteria would be that the latch does not open unless you pull on it. Engineers might explain how much force you need to pull on it with.

The second part is defining the constraints. *Constraints* are the limits on the design. Constraints include limits on time, materials, or costs. A NASA engineer might design a shuttle to carry astronauts. But the shuttle needs to take less than one year to build. So, the time it takes to build is one constraint.

These students are observing that their box comes open when they shake it. So, they are defining a problem. Then they will design a solution using their knowledge of magnets.

Developing and Using Models

Models in science represent ideas in the real world. Diagrams and mathematical representations are examples of models. So are physical copies and computer simulations. Models are not perfect copies of the ideas they represent. They make some parts of the concept clearer. But they make some parts less clear.

A Spring Toy Model

One example of a model is a spring toy being pushed back and forth. It can represent a sound wave. This model makes the motion of the wave clear. It shows that matter compresses together in crests and spreads apart in troughs. But it does not show that sound waves traveling through air are moving through many particles. It also does not show that sound waves spread out in all directions. Still, the model helps show basic properties of sound waves like amplitude and wavelength.

These students are using a spring toy to model sound waves. They will use the properties they observe in this model to describe other kinds of waves.

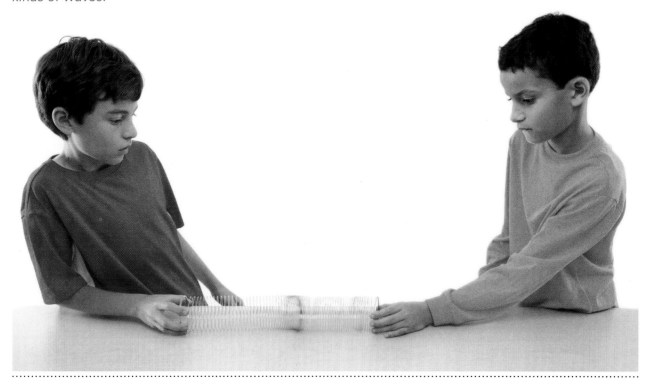

A Pinhole Camera Model

A pinhole camera is another example of a model. It can represent the human eye. It shows that light passes through the opening in the front of an eye and that the light is projected onto a screen in the back of the eye. It also shows that the image projected is upside down.

Many human eye functions can be investigated using a pinhole camera. However, a pinhole camera is unlike an eye in other ways. It is not made of the same materials as a human eye. It is also not filled with liquid. Instead of being round like an eye, it is a cylinder. And it does not have a lens in the front.

But the pinhole camera model is useful for understanding certain properties of the human eye. It shows how light enters the eye. It also shows how the light projects onto the back of the eye. But, as with all models, it is not a perfect representation. So, it is not useful for studying things like the specific structure of the eye.

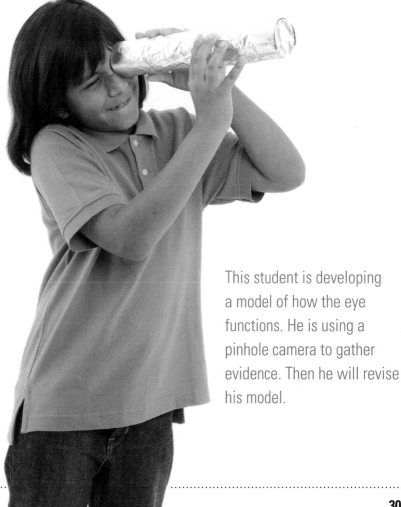

This student is developing a model of how the eye functions. He is using a pinhole camera to gather evidence. Then he will revise his model.

Planning and Carrying Out Investigations

Investigations are one of the main ways scientists and engineers gather evidence. This evidence supports their claims. Scientists use the evidence to construct and defend explanations and to answer questions. Engineers use evidence to identify problems or to decide between different solutions to the same problem. They also use it to determine how they can improve a solution.

Planning an Investigation

One of the key steps in successful investigation is planning. There are many different parts to plan. Here are a few important questions to ask while planning an investigation:

- What question am I trying to answer?
- What are my expected results?
- What data is the best evidence to answer my question?
- How will I collect and record my data?
- What errors are likely to occur during my investigation? And how can I prevent them?
- What safety issues do I need to think about?

These students are investigating how the height from which they drop a ball affects how high it bounces. They will use the data they gather to predict how high the ball will bounce in the future.

The Variables of an Investigation

The easiest way to do decide what data to collect in an investigation is to consider all the variables. A *variable* is a factor that can affect the outcome. Suppose you are testing a water filter. One variable affecting the test is the amount of water poured into the filter. Another is how quickly the water is poured.

Most investigations test the effect of one variable on the outcome. You might test how the rate of water being poured into the filter affects the effectiveness of the filter. In order to test just one variable, all the other variables must be the same in every test. So, you need to make sure you use the same amount of water and dirt in each test. But you need to change the rate that you pour water.

In most investigations, there are some variables that cannot be kept the same in every test. For example, the person holding the filter might shake a little bit. This makes the results change. So, scientists often repeat the same experiment many times. Each time is called a *trial*. They look at the average, or usual, results of the experiments. The more trials they do, the more confident they are that their results are correct.

These students are testing a design for a water filter. They consider variables to make sure their results are accurate.

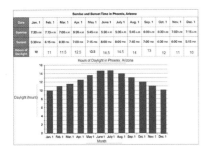

A bar graph can show patterns in data.

These students are analyzing measurements of the lengths of shadows during different times of the day. They will use their data to explain how the position of the sun affects the length of shadows.

Analyzing and Interpreting Data

Once you complete an investigation, you often have a data table full of numbers. But you might have pictures or words instead. How can you tell what all that *data*, or pieces of information, means?

Analyzing and interpreting data is the process of identifying patterns in data. It lets scientists turn their data into evidence. The evidence then supports their claim. Analyzing data might include graphing it to see a pattern. For example, you might make a bar graph that shows the length of shadows during different times of day. A graph will show the pattern of shadows better than a data table will. Analyzing data might also include identifying relationships between variables. Suppose you grow a bean plant. You might find that the plant grows 3 cm each week. Analyzing your data shows the relationship between height of the plant and time.

Scientists use many different methods to analyze data. They use many types of graphs. They also use mathematical formulas and tools. They compare data between trials and experiments. They even compare their data to data gathered by other scientists. They often use computers to help them find patterns in the data.

Finding Patterns with Graphs

Scientists use many different kinds of graphs and charts. These help them to find patterns. They use bar graphs to show how much of the data fits into a category. They might measure how much rain fell each month during a year. They could use a bar graph to show the amount of rain that fell in each month. The bar graph would show what parts of the year had more rain than other parts.

Line plots show a relationship between two variables. Line plots have two axes. There is one variable on each axis. They show how a change in one variable affects the other variable. A line plot might show how many hours of sunlight there are each day of the year.

These students are comparing the data each group gathered about rainfall in different years. They are looking for patterns in the rainfall during different seasons.

Using Mathematics and Computational Thinking

Mathematics plays a key role in science and engineering. Measurements and calculations provide evidence to support scientific explanations. The evidence can also disprove scientific explanations. Engineers use measurements to communicate their designs.

Using Measurements

One example of how measurements are useful in science is when you weigh things. You might measure the weight of cream before and after shaking it into butter. Without measurements, you may guess that the cream is about the same weight as the butter and buttermilk together. But by measuring, you can say with confidence that they are the same weight.

This student is measuring the weight of butter and buttermilk that she made by shaking cream. She also measured the weight of the cream. She will compare the weights before and after the change.

Graphing Data

Graphing is another example of how mathematics supports science. Often, scientists gather lots of data in tables. But it is difficult to see any patterns in the data. But when they graph it, they can see patterns more easily. These patterns suggest relationships between different factors. The data can then support explanations.

Graphing data also helps engineers. They use it to decide between different possible designs. They might test the amount of water several materials can absorb. Then they could decide which material will make the best sponge. By graphing the results of different designs using the same test, they can tell which design works best. Or they can see the strengths and weaknesses of each design.

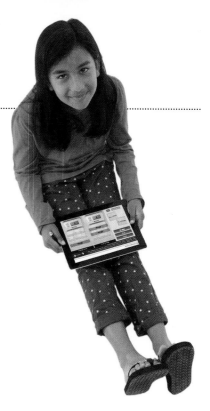

This student learned that the weight of substances does not change. She is using this knowledge to predict how much an ice cube will weigh after it melts.

1. Use the data in the table to create a line graph showing how high above the horizon these four constellations are at different times of year in the Northern Hemisphere.

- Give the graph a title.
- Label the x-axis "Month."
- Label the y-axis "Altitude (degrees)."
- Graph and connect all of the points, using a different color for each constellation
- Add a key.

	Jan.	Feb.	Mar.	Apr.	May	June	July	Aug.	Sep.	Oct.	Nov.	Dec.
Leo	11°	35°	53°	62°	50°	28°	6°	0°	0°	0°	0°	0°
Scorpius	0°	0°	0°	12°	22°	21°	10°	0°	0°	0°	0°	0°
Pisces	5°	0°	0°	0°	0°	0°	0°	21°	42°	53°	46°	28°
Orion	44°	36°	19°	0°	0°	0°	0°	0°	0°	0°	19°	36°

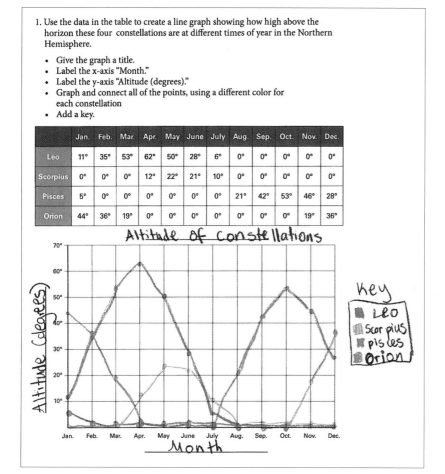

Graphing data helps scientists and engineers see patterns in their data.

Constructing Explanations and Designing Solutions

The main goal of science is to construct explanations for things observed in the world. An explanation is almost always a claim about the world. It can be a claim about two variables. For example, a claim could be moths with camouflage patterns that match their background are more likely to survive than moths with camouflage patterns that do not match their background.

Scientists Construct Explanations

While constructing explanations, scientists often investigate to gather data. Then they analyze the data. Often they use mathematics to do this. They usually use models to help construct their explanation. They use evidence to argue that their explanation is correct.

After constructing an explanation, scientists may ask more questions to clarify the explanation. They may have to change their models. Scientists also often communicate their explanations to other scientists. They might do this by writing papers or giving presentations.

These students are using evidence from their investigation of moth camouflage to explain how characteristics can give advantages to members of a species.

One problem is converting energy stored in a battery into energy carried by light. So, these students design multiple solutions. They are using scientific ideas they learned about energy, electric current, and light to solve the problem.

Engineers Design Solutions

The main goal of engineering is to design solutions to problems. But the process has many of the same steps. Engineers still have to test their solutions. They also use evidence to show that their solution is the best one to solve the problem. After designing solutions, engineers often revise them. They ask questions about how they can improve the solution. Or they might ask what other related problems need to be solved. They communicate their solutions in similar ways as scientists.

The process of designing solutions has several steps. After defining the problem, engineers brainstorm many possible solutions. They compare the different possible solutions to decide which one is most likely to succeed. They may use models of the solution to compare them. After building the solution, engineers think about how the solution could be improved. They repeat this process several times to try to develop the best solution.

Engaging in Argument from Evidence

One process in scientific reasoning is engaging in argument from evidence. Arguments help scientists decide which explanation best fits the evidence. They help engineers decide which design solution best meets the criteria.

A Scientific Argument

There are three main pieces in a *scientific argument*. The first is a *claim*, which is the explanation that the argument supports. The argument claims that this explanation is correct. It is often a simple statement like "wolves eat meat."

The second piece is *evidence* that the claim is correct. This is the observations or data that support that claim. Evidence can be taken from investigations, research, or a model. For instance, one piece of evidence may be that "all wolves have sharp teeth."

The third piece is reasoning that connects the evidence to the claim. *Reasoning* explains why the evidence supports the claim. All evidence should have reasoning. Consider the example of wolves' teeth. The reasoning could be "animals that eat meat need sharp teeth for tearing the meat, but animals that eat plants need flat teeth for grinding plants."

This student is observing different kinds of animals' teeth. He will use his observations as evidence in an argument about how wolves and horses use their teeth to survive.

Obtaining, Evaluating, and Communicating Information

It is very rare for scientists and engineers to work alone. Almost all scientists work in teams, so they often communicate their investigations with each other. Many scientists are also often working on answering similar questions. This means that scientists share their results and information with each other.

How Scientists Obtain Information

Scientists make their results available in many ways so that others can learn from them. One way they do this is by writing up their results. Another is by presenting their research. In an investigation, you might present your research to your classmates.

While reading other people's research, scientists make sure that the information is reliable. They check to see if the data supports their explanations. They read about the methods used by the other scientists and look for possible errors. They also look to see whether the results of the experiment described match the results of similar experiments.

These students used a reliable source to find information about climates in different regions of the world. They are combining the information on one world map.

Using Science and Engineering Tools

The Metric System

The *metric system* is a system of measurement. It is used by scientists and engineers all over the world. Using the same system of measurement makes it easier to communicate scientific findings and engineering designs between different parts of the world.

Base Units

The metric system has several base units used for making different kinds of measurements. Here are a few of the most important ones:

Measurement	Base Unit	Symbol
Length	Meter	m
Volume	Liter	L
Mass or Weight	Gram	g
Time	Second	s
Temperature	Degree Celsius	°C

Prefixes

This chart shows you the prefixes of different units in the metric system. Each prefix makes a base unit larger or smaller.

The metric system also has prefixes that indicate different amounts of each unit. Adding a prefix to a base unit makes a new unit, which is made larger or smaller than the base unit by multiplying by a certain factor of 10. Each prefix represents a different factor of 10.

Prefix	Symbol	Word	Decimal	Factor of 10
kilo	k	Thousand	1,000	10^3
centi	c	Hundredth	0.01	1/100
milli	m	Thousandth	0.001	1/1,000

Using a Hand Lens

Hand lenses are tools for making observations. They make objects and living things viewed through them appear larger. This allows scientists to see parts of an object that they cannot see with just their eyes. It helps scientist see more details of an object.

To use a hand lens:

- hold the lens close to your face in between the object you want to magnify and yourself. The object should appear blurry.

- slowly move the hand lens away from your face. When the object is no longer blurry, it is said to be "in focus."

- find the position where the object is in focus, and hold the hand lens still while you observe the object.

This student is holding the hand lens the right distance from his face to keep the leaf in focus. It helps him see the structures that make up the leaf in more detail.

Measuring Length

Small lengths and distances are measured in centimeters. Larger lengths and distances are measured in meters or kilometers. There are other units to measure lengths and distances. Some are even smaller than centimeters or larger than kilometers.

To measure lengths and distances, you can use a ruler. Rulers have marks that show length on them. Each mark is the same distance from the mark before it. The marks are usually one centimeter or one inch apart. Many have centimeters on one side and inches on the other side.

To use a ruler:

- find the 0 cm mark on the ruler.

- line it up with one end of the length you are measuring.

- hold the ruler along the length.

- find the centimeter mark nearest to the other end of the length.

- the number on that mark is the length measurement you should record.

Remember to record what units you used!

To measure length, you lay a ruler next to the length you are measuring. Find the 0 mark and the other end, and then record the length and units. This drawer is 20 cm wide.

Measuring Temperature

Temperature is measured in degrees Celsius. You can measure temperature with a *thermometer*. Many thermometers are glass tubes with red liquid inside. As the temperature increases, the liquid expands and fills more of the tube. The thermometer has marks on it that show the temperature. Since these thermometers are made of glass, you have to be careful while using them to be sure not to break them.

Digital thermometers have a metal tip that you put in the substance you are measuring. They display the temperature on a screen.

To read a thermometer with a glass tube:

- hold it near the top where there is not liquid.

- hold it so the top of the liquid is level with your eye.

- find the mark that is closest to the top of the liquid.

- record the temperature indicated by the mark.

Remember to record the units your thermometer uses!

This ice water is 0° C. You can see that the top of the red liquid is exactly at the 0° C mark.

Measuring Liquid Volume

Liquid volumes are measured in liters. Smaller volumes might be measured in milliliters or fluid ounces. There are 1000 milliliters in 1 liter.

A *graduated cylinder* is a tool that accurately measures the volume of liquids. It is a thin cylinder with marks on the side. It shows the volume of liquid there is in the cylinder below the mark.

To accurately measure volume with a graduated cylinder:

- make sure the cylinder is completely empty and dry.
- fill it with the liquid you want to measure.
- set the cylinder down on a flat surface.
- make sure the liquid is not splashing back and forth.
- crouch down so your eye is level with the top of the liquid.
- the liquid should be curved slightly, so it is lower in the middle than at the sides.
- find which mark is closest to the bottom of the curve. That is the volume of the liquid in the graduated cylinder.

Remember to record the units you used to measure the volume!

This graduated cylinder is full of liquid. Find the bottom of the curve in the top of the liquid. Which mark is it closest to? There are 96 mL of liquid in the graduated cylinder.

Measuring Mass or Weight

Small amounts of mass or weight are measured in grams. Larger amounts of mass or weight are measured in kilograms. There are 1000 grams in a kilogram.

Using a Balance Scale With Two Pans

You can measure mass or weight using a *balance scale*. Some balance scales have two pans.

These weights can be used with a balance scale.

To use a balance scale:

- put the object you want to measure in one pan. That pan should sink down.

- put weights in the other pan. You should know the mass of each of the weights.

- add weights to the second side until the two sides are balanced. So, neither side sinks down.

- add up all the masses on the second side. Their total mass is equal to the mass of the object on the first side.

To measure the mass or weight of this orange, first you would put the orange on one pan of the balance scale. Then you would put weights in the other pan. You would add and take away weights until the pans are balanced.

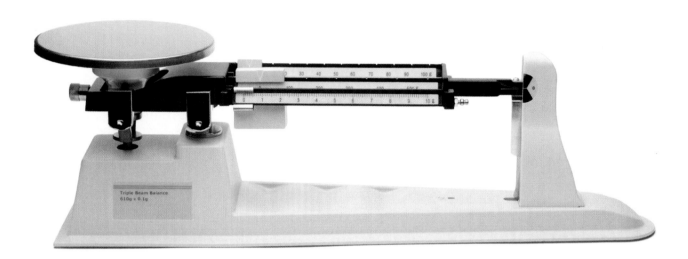

A triple beam balance scale uses one pan and three beams to measure the weight of objects. The beams measure hundreds, tens, and ones.

Using a Triple Beam Balance Scale

A triple beam balance scale is another kind of balance scale. It only has one pan, which is where you put the object you want to weigh. There are three sliders. One measures grams in hundreds, one measures them in tens, and one measures them in ones. There are also two lines, one on the beam with the weights and one on the frame. When the lines are lined up with each other, the scale is balanced.

An apple can weigh about 100 grams. But do all apples weigh 100 grams? Probably not. How heavy are different apples? To find out, you could carry out an investigation using a triple beam balance. You might collect some apples and measure their weights. You would place one apple on the pan of the balance at a time. Then you would find the weight and record it in a table. Finally, you would weigh some other apples and analyze your data.

To measure the weight of an object with a triple beam balance:

- place the object on the pan.
- slide the hundreds weight until the line on the beam falls below the line on the frame.
- slide the weight one notch back. The line on the beam should rise up above the line on the frame.
- slide the tens weight until the line falls down again.
- slide the weight one notch back. The line on the beam should rise up above the line on the frame.
- slide the ones weight until the beam is balanced, and the line on the beam is lined up with the line on the frame. Move the ones weight a little at a time to make sure your measurement is accurate.
- add up all of the weights to find the total weight of the object.

Remember to record the units you used!

Add up the weights to find the weight of the object. The scale reads 101.4 g.

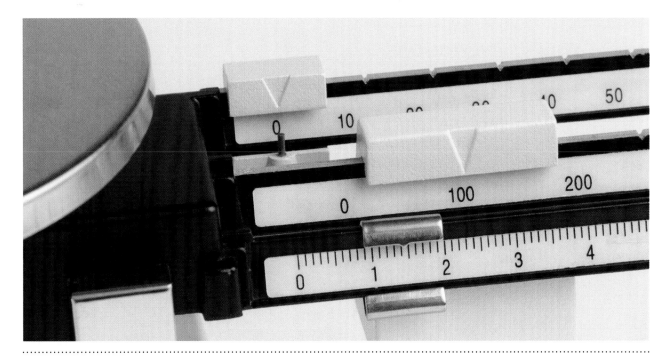

A

adaptation　A behavior or body part that helps an organism survive and reproduce in its environment.

air mass　A large body of air in the atmosphere of the same temperature and humidity.

anemometer　A tool that measures wind speed.

atmosphere　The blanket of air that surrounds Earth.

B

bacteria　A type of tiny living thing that cannot be seen without a microscope.

balanced forces　Forces that together do not cause a change in motion.

behavior　An action that an organism does.

blizzard　A long-lasting snowstorm with a lot of falling or blowing snow.

C

camouflage　When an animal's color makes it hard to see against a similarly colored background.

climate　An area's typical weather over a long period of time.

D

data　Pieces of information about something, such as facts or measurements. For example, if you write down your daytime temperatures for a week, you are recording data.

desert　An area with a dry climate.

drought　When not enough rain falls for a long period of time.

dust storm　A storm that forms when strong winds pick up large amounts of dry soil. This forms big, blowing clouds of dust.

E

electric force　A push or pull between objects that have an electric charge.

electromagnet　A magnet that can turn on or off.

endangered　In danger of going extinct. There are few members left alive when a species is endangered.

environment　All the living and nonliving things that surround an organism.

equator　An imaginary line around Earth, midway between the North and South poles.

evaporation When a liquid water changes to water vapor.

exoskeleton A hard body covering that protects soft inside parts of some animals.

extinct Having no living members. When a species is extinct, all members of that species have died.

F

flower A part of some plants where seeds are made.

force A push or pull.

fossil The remaining pieces or trace of an organism that lived long ago.

front Where one air mass meets another air mass. Storms and clouds often form at fronts.

fruit The part of a plant that surrounds and protects a seed.

G

genes Inherited information that tells offspring what traits to have.

gravity A force that pulls down.

H

humidity The amount of water vapor in the air.

hurricane A large, spinning storm with strong winds that forms over a tropical ocean.

I

infer To use evidence to draw a conclusion. Scientists infer facts about animals and their environments from fossils.

inherited trait A characteristic passed from a parent to its offspring.

invertebrate An animal without a backbone, like insects, lobsters, and octopuses.

L

larva The second stage in the life cycle of some invertebrates. A larva becomes a pupa that goes through rapid metamorphosis.

learned behavior A trait an organism learns over its lifetime.

life cycle The pattern of changes that a member of a species goes through during its lifetime.

life span   The typical amount of time that most members of a species live, from birth to death.

lightning rod   A metal rod connected by a wire to the ground that helps prevent lightning from striking houses or buildings.

M

magnetic force   A push or pull between two or more magnets or between a magnet and certain types of metal.

mate   An animal that can reproduce with another animal of the same species.

metamorphosis   A large change in body shape during the life cycle of some animal species.

meteorologist   A scientist who studies weather.

motion   A change in the position of an object.

N

natural resource   A useful material that comes from the natural environment.

nymph   The second stage in the life cycle of many insects. These insects go through gradual metamorphosis.

O

offspring   The young organisms that result when adult organisms reproduce.

organism   A living thing.

P

permanent magnet   A magnet that you cannot turn on or off.

position   An object's location compared to its surroundings.

precipitation   Water that falls to the ground in the form of rain, snow, or sleet.

predict   To use what you know to tell what might happen in the future.

prey   An animal that is hunted and eaten.

R

radar   A tool that is used to find far away objects in the air and measure their distance or speed.

rain gauge   A tool that measures rainfall.

rainforest   A forest environment that receives a very large amount of rain.

reproduce   To make more of the same species of an organism.

S

seed   A small, protected part of a plant that can grow into an adult offspring.

social animal   An animal that lives in a group with others of its kind in order to meet its needs.

species   A group of living things of the same kind.

static electricity   The effects of an imbalance of positive and negative charges.

survive   To stay alive.

T

temperature   How warm or cool something is.

thermometer   A tool that measures temperature.

thunderstorm   A strong storm that brings wind, rain, thunder, and lightning.

tornado   A dangerous and powerful mass of spinning air.

trait   A characteristic that a living thing has.

U

unbalanced forces   Forces that together cause a change in motion.

V

vertebrate   An animal with a backbone.

W

water vapor   Water in the air that you cannot see.

weather station   A set of equipment that measures temperature and other weather information. They normally take these measurements automatically several times a day.

weather   What the atmosphere is like at a certain time and place.

wetlands   Low, soggy areas where land and water meet.

wildfire   A large fire in a forest or grassland.

wind vane   A tool that measures the direction wind comes from.

CREDITS

stock **95 (#2):** ASSOCIATED PRESS **95 (#3):** Copyright/Edith Held/Corbis/AP Images **95 (#4):** BanksPhotos/iStockphoto **96:** Thinkstock **97:** NASA

Unit 2, Lesson 3
98: Christopher Meder/Dreamstime **99 L:** Alamy **99 R:** Blend Images/Alamy **100:** PhotoAlto/Alix Minde/Getty Images **101:** General Wesc/Flikr **102:** Radius Images/Alamy **103 (#1):** Alamy **103 (#2):** General Wesc/Flikr **103 (#3):** Radius Images/Alamy **104:** NASA **105 T:** SeanPavonePhoto/Shutterstock **105 B:** NOAA/NASA/GOES **106:** NASA/Dimitri Gerondidakis **107:** Photo Researchers Inc/Getty Images

Unit 2, Lesson 4
108: Dan Van Den Broeke/Dreamstime **109 T:** Fireflyphoto/Dreamstime **110:** Thinkstock **111 B:** Corbis/SuperStock **111 T:** Newlight/Dreamstime **112 L:** Dan Van Den Broeke/Dreamstime **112 R:** Lourens Smak/Alamy **113:** Flikr **114:** iStockphoto **115 (#2):** Thinkstock **115 (#3):** Corbis/SuperStock **115 (#4):** Lourens Smak/Alamy **115 (#5):** Flikr **115 (#6):** iStockphoto **116:** Thinkstock **117:** 1000 Words/Shutterstock **118:** Hungchungchih/Dreamstime **119:** Martin Bond/Photo Researchers, Inc.

Unit 2, Lesson 5
120: Viktor Levi/Dreamstime **122:** Ivary Inc./Alamy **123 B:** GIPhotoStock/Science Source **123 T:** Saturated/istockphoto **124:** Thinkstock **125 (#2):** Ivary Inc./Alamy **125 (#3):** GIPhotoStock/Science Source **125 (#4):** Thinkstock **126:** Thinkstock **127:** karrapavan/Shutterstock **128:** Mark Newman/Getty Images **129 T:** imagebroker.net/SuperStock **129 B:** Shutterstock

Unit 3, Unit Opener
130-131: A. T. Willett/Alamy **133 TR:** Cultura Creative (RF)/Alamy **133 BR:** Showface/Dreamstime **133 L:** Monkey Business Images/Shutterstock

Unit 3, Lesson 1
134: Thinkstock **135:** NASA **136 T:** Thinkstock **136 B:** Thinkstock **137 B:** Thinkstock **137 T:** Thinkstock **138:** Thinkstock **139 (#1):** NASA **139 (#2):** Thinkstock **139 (#3):** Thinkstock **139 (#4):** Thinkstock **140:** Thinkstock **141:** Gary Szatkowski **142 B:** ASSOCIATED PRESS **142 T:** Thinkstock **143:** Zhukovsky/Dreamstime

Unit 3, Lesson 2
144: Thinkstock **145:** Thinkstock **146 B:** Thinkstock **146 T:** Thinkstock **147 T:** Thinkstock **147 B:** Ryan McGinnis/Alamy **149 (#1):** Thinkstock **149 (#2):** Thinkstock **150:** Thinkstock **151:** ASSOCIATED PRESS **152:** Marzanna Syncerz/Dreamstime **153:** ASSOCIATED PRESS

Unit 3, Lesson 3
154: Phil MacD Photography/Shutterstock **156 T:** Thinkstock **156 B:** Thinkstock **157 B:** Thinkstock **157 T:** Thinkstock **159 (#2):** Thinkstock **159 (#3):** Thinkstock **160:** Thinkstock **161 L:** Radekdrewek/Dreamstime **161 R:** Neirfy/Dreamstime **162:** Juraj Kovacik/Dreamstime **163:** Construction Photography/Alamy

Unit 3, Lesson 4
164: Jaco Janse Van Rensburg/Dreamstime **165 T:** Thinkstock **166 L:** Thinkstock **166 C:** Thinkstock **166 R:** Thinkstock **167 B:** Fireflyphoto/Dreamstime **167 T:** age fotostock/Alamy **168 L:** Thinkstock **168 R:** Linda Bair/Dreamstime **169 (#1):** Thinkstock **169 (#2):** Thinkstock **169 (#3):** Fireflyphoto/Dreamstime **169 (#4):** Thinkstock **169 (#4):** Linda Bair/Dreamstime **170:** Thinkstock **171 B:** Thinkstock **171 T:** Thinkstock **172:** MARIANA BAZO/Reuters/Corbis **173 B:** RGB Ventures LLC dba SuperStock/Alamy **173 T:** Carnegie Mellon University

Unit 3, Lesson 5
174: Thinkstock **175 B:** Thinkstock **175 T:** Thinkstock **178 T:** National Science Foundation **178 B:** Thinkstock **179 B:** IM_photo/Shutterstock **179 T:** Peter Menzel/Science Source **181 (#1):** Thinkstock **181 (#3):** Thinkstock **182:** Dreamstime **183:** iStockphoto **184:** Nancy Bauer/Shutterstock **185:** iStockphoto

Unit 3, Lesson 6
186: Shutterstock **188 L:** Shutterstock **188 R:** Oleg Znamenskiy/Shutterstock **189 R:** Thinkstock **189 L:** Thinkstock **190:** Thinkstock **191 (#2):** Thinkstock **191 (#3):** Thinkstock **192:** Rinus Baak/Dreamstime **193:** Thinkstock **194 B:** Jorge Salcedo/Dreamstime **194 T:** iStockphoto **195:** Dreamstime

Unit 3, Lesson 7
196: Todd Shoemake/Shutterstock **197 B:** ASSOCIATED PRESS **197 T:** ASSOCIATED PRESS **198 B:** Thinkstock **199:** Thinkstock **200:** Todd Shoemake/Shutterstock **201:** ASSOCIATED PRESS **202 B:** ASSOCIATED PRESS **202 T:** ASSOCIATED PRESS **203 (#1):** ASSOCIATED PRESS **203 (#2):** Thinkstock **203 (#3):** Thinkstock **203 (#4):** Todd Shoemake/Shutterstock **203 (#5):** ASSOCIATED PRESS **203 (#6):** ASSOCIATED PRESS **204:** Thinkstock

Unit 3, Lesson 8
206: Shutterstock **209 T:** Alexander Kuguchin/Shutterstock **209 B:** Alexander Kuguchin/Shutterstock **210:** ASSOCIATED PRESS **211 (#2):** Alexander Kuguchin/Shutterstock **211 (#3):** ASSOCIATED PRESS **212:** By Bureau of Land Management [CC-BY-2.0 (http://creativecommons.org/licenses/by/2.0)], via Wikimedia Commons **213 B:** Harris Shiffman/Dreamstime **213 T:** Dreamstime **214:** NOAA **215:** Thinkstock

CREDITS

Unit 4, Unit Opener
216-217: Els Jooren/Shutterstock **219 TR:** Rodho/Dreamstime **219 L:** iStockphoto **219 BR:** Mykola Velychko/Dreamstime

Unit 4, Lesson 1
220: Countrymama/Dreamstime **221 T:** Koi88/Dreamstime **221 R:** Sean Pavone/Dreamstime **221 L:** Nutthawit Wiangya/Dreamstime **222 L:** Brian Kushner/Dreamstime **222 R:** Brian Kushner/Dreamstime **223:** Len44ik/Dreamstime **224:** Szefei/Dreamstime **225:** Wayne Mckown/Dreamstime **226:** Isselee/Dreamstime **226:** Dan Breckwoldt/Dreamstime **226:** Beeldphoto/Dreamstime **226:** Erik Lam/Dreamstime **226 R:** Isselee/Dreamstime **226 L:** Eric Isselee/123rf **227 (#1):** Koi88/Dreamstime **227 (#2):** Brian Kushner/Dreamstime **227 (#3):** Len44ik/Dreamstime **227 (#4):** Szefei/Dreamstime **227 (#5):** Eric Isselee/123rf **228:** Four Oaks/Shutterstock **229:** Thinkstock **230:** Nicram Sabod/Shutterstock **231 L:** KeithSzafranski/iStockphoto **231 R:** Eric Gevaert/Dreamstime

Unit 4, Lesson 2
232: Byelikova/Dreamstime **233:** Snicol24/Dreamstime **234:** 12qwerty/Dreamstime **235:** Darrinhenry/Dreamstime **236:** Andrea Borsani/Dreamstime **237 (#1):** Snicol24/Dreamstime **237 (#2):** 12qwerty/Dreamstime **237 (#3):** Darrinhenry/Dreamstime **237 (#4):** Andrea Borsani/Dreamstime **238:** Thinkstock **239:** Shutterstock **240:** iStockphoto **241:** Maxim Kiryushin/Dreamstime

Unit 4, Lesson 3
242: Heinz Effner/Dreamstime **243 R:** Anourina/Dreamstime **243 L:** Milous Chab/Dreamstime **244 L:** Romangorielov/Dreamstime **244 R:** Thinkstock **245 R:** Jolanta Dabrowska/Dreamstime **245 L:** Audines/Dreamstime **246:** Lucy Cherniak/Dreamstime **247 (#1):** Anourina/Dreamstime **247 (#2):** Romangorielov/Dreamstime **247 (#3):** Jolanta Dabrowska/Dreamstime **247 (#4):** Lucy Cherniak/Dreamstime **248:** Lunamarina/Dreamstime **249 B:** iStockphoto **249 T:** Capture Light/Shutterstock **250 L:** Kippy Spilker/Dreamstime **250 C:** Shutterstock **250 R:** Krissi Lundgren/Dreamstime **251:** Goldenkb/Dreamstime

Unit 4, Lesson 4
252: Stuart G Porter/Shutterstock **253:** Odm/Dreamstime **254:** Teodor Ostojic/Dreamstime **255:** Javarman/Dreamstime **256:** Egon Zitter/Dreamstime **257:** Fullempty/Dreamstime **258:** Derkien/Dreamstime **259 (#1):** Odm/Dreamstime **259 (#2):** Teodor Ostojic/Dreamstime **259 (#3):** Javarman/Dreamstime **259 (#4):** Egon Zitter/Dreamstime **259 (#5):** Fullempty/Dreamstime **259 (#6):** Derkien/Dreamstime **260:** Reimar 3/Alamy **261:** Grand Canyon NPS **262:** Ray Warren Animals/Alamy **263:** Photoshot Holdings Ltd/Alamy

Unit 4, Lesson 5
264: ValentynVolkov/iStockphoto **265:** Wam1975/Dreamstime **269 (#1):** Wam1975/Dreamstime **270:** Pete Oxford/Minden Pictures/Corbis **271 T:** Anita Van Kol/Dreamstime **271 B:** iStockphoto

Unit 4, Lesson 6
272: London Taxidermy/Alamy **273:** Thinkstock **274 L:** Kheng Ho Toh/Dreamstime **274 R:** Laschi/Dreamstime **276:** Daburke/Dreamstime **277:** IrinaK/Shutterstock **279 (#1):** Thinkstock **279 (#2):** Laschi/Dreamstime **279 (#3):** Daburke/Dreamstime **280:** Karl Ammann/Corbis **281:** Daniel Bellhouse/Dreamstime **282:** Nick Biemans/Dreamstime **283:** Thinkstock

Unit 4, Lesson 7
284: Mark Bridger/Shutterstock **285 L:** Benjamin Simeneta/Dreamstime **285 R:** Thinkstock **287:** Amanda Melones/Dreamstime **288:** iliuta goean/Shutterstock **291 (#1):** Benjamin Simeneta/Dreamstime **291 (#3):** iliuta goean/Shutterstock **292:** Images & Stories/Alamy

Back Matter
295: Caro/Alamy **296:** Thinkstock **297:** Radius Images/Alamy **299 T:** weerayut ranmai/Shutterstock **313:** Cultura Creative Alamy **314:** Thinkstock **315:** Adam Hart-Davis/Science Source **316:** Thinkstock **317 T:** Asaf Eliason/Shutterstock **317 B:** JIANG HONGYAN/Shutterstock **320:** Thinkstock **318 T:** Martin Shields/Alamy **318 B:** Shutterstock **319:** Martin Shields/Alamy